Edinburgh

A Very Peculiar History™

Athens of the North – without the heat!

'The haughty Dun-Edin, the Queen of the North;
There learning shall flourish, and liberty smile,
The awe of the world, and the pride of the isle ...'

James Hogg, *The Queen's Wake*, 1813

For Andy, as always
FMacD

Editor: Victoria England
Editorial assistants: Rob Walker, Mark Williams

Published in Great Britain in MMXIV by
Book House, an imprint of
The Salariya Book Company Ltd
25 Marlborough Place, Brighton BN1 1UB
www.salariya.com
www.book-house.co.uk

HB ISBN-13: 978-1-908973-82-5

1 3 5 7 9 8 6 4 2

A CIP catalogue record for this book is available
from the British Library.
Printed and bound in Dubai.
Printed on paper from sustainable sources.

Visit
www.salariya.com
for our online catalogue and
free interactive web books.

Edinburgh
A Very Peculiar History™

Athens of the North – without the heat!

Written by
Fiona Macdonald

Created and designed by
David Salariya

BOOK HOUSE
a SALARIYA imprint

'Edinburgh isn't so much a city,
more a way of life...'

Novelist Ian Rankin

Contents

Putting Edinburgh on the map

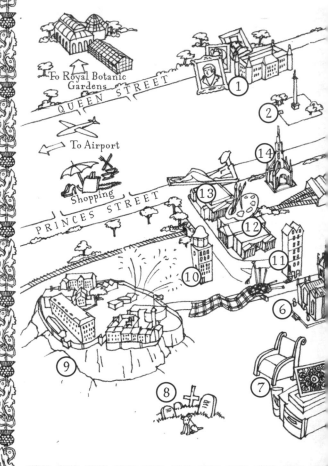

To Royal Botanic Gardens

QUEEN STREET

To Airport

Shopping

PRINCES STREET

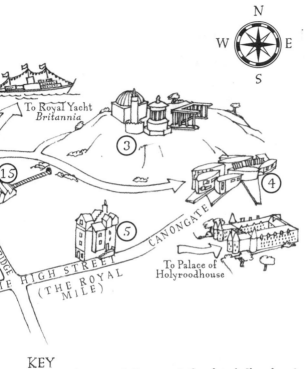

KEY
1 National Portrait Gallery
2 St Andrew's Square
3 Calton Hill
4 Scottish Parliament
5 John Knox House
6 St Giles High Kirk, also
  known as St Giles Cathedral
7 National Museum of
  Scotland
8 Greyfriar's Churchyard
9 Edinburgh Castle
10 Camera Obscura
11 Gladstone's Land
12 National Gallery of
  Scotland
13 Royal Scottish Academy
14 Scott Monument
15 Waverley Station

Putting Edinburgh on the map: A tourist's view

So much to see! So little time! According to official statistics, the average visitor to Edinburgh spends only a few days in the city. So what are the sights most likely to catch the eye of a busy tourist, in the Old Town, the New Town and in Edinburgh's surroundings? Hold on tight – our whirlwind tour is about to begin!

1. **National Portrait Gallery** – the world's first purpose-built gallery of likenesses. All Scottish life is here! The building, completed in 1896, is famous for its carved frieze of famous Scots.
2. **St Andrew's Square** – named after Scotland's patron saint, this is one of the glories of the New Town. Building started in 1772, and the square soon became home to the rich and famous, then offices for top finance companies. The tall pillar commemorates Henry Dundas, Viscount Melville (1742–1811), one of Scotland's most successful – and controversial – politicians.
3. **Calton Hill** – a high site for many great monuments. You can read more about it on pages 24 and 25.
4. **Scottish Parliament** – designed by Catalan architect Enric Miralles, and completed, vastly over budget, in 2004. The outside has been criticised. The interior is wonderful.
5. **John Knox House** – one of Edinburgh's oldest surviving buildings, dating from 1490. Protestant preacher John Knox is said to have lived here. He didn't; his home was in Warriston Close, nearby.
6. **St Giles Cathedral** – more correctly, the High Kirk of St Giles. There has been a church on this site for over 900 years. The present building, with its unusual crown spire (1495), dates from around 1385. John Knox *was* here; he was appointed Minister in 1559.

7. **National Museum of Scotland** – home to many Scottish cultural icons, from the Lewis Chessmen to the 'Maiden' guillotine and Dolly the Sheep (see page 177).
8. **Greyfriar's Churchyard** – read about this on pages 180–181.
9. **Edinburgh Castle** – claims to be 'Edinburgh's most famous tourist attraction'. The Castle Esplanade hosts the annual Edinburgh Tattoo: music and marching by international armies.
10. **Camera Obscura** – a tall tower containing a 'pinhole camera' that projects an image of the city on a screen. Installed on present site by pioneer sociologist Patrick Geddes in 1892.
11. **Gladstone's Land** – typical tall Edinburgh tenement block, dating from around 1550. Splendidly restored by the National Trust for Scotland.
12. **National Gallery of Scotland** – designed in classical style by architect William Playfair, and opened in 1859. Old Master and Impressionist paintings, fine landscapes, Scottish portraits.
13. **Royal Scottish Academy** – another stunning building by Playfair, completed in 1826. Now displays modern art.
14. **Scott Monument** – unmissable, and, if you're feeling fit, you can climb up inside. Find out more on page 150.
15. **Waverley Station** – the only British railway terminus named after a novel. (By Sir Walter Scott, of course). There's been a station on the site since the 1840s. Today it handles over 22 million passengers per year.

Royal Botanic Gardens – beautiful and useful. A centre for the scientific study of plants. Originally founded in Edinburgh in 1670, it moved to Inverleith in 1820.

Royal Yacht *Brittania* – built in Clydebank, Scotland 1954, decommissioned 1997, and now moored at Leith. You can take a tour.

Holyroodhouse – royal palace since c. 1500. Today, the Queen visits for around one week per year.

Edinburgh Airport – at first a military base, converted for civilian use in 1971, and now Scotland's busiest airport, with over 9 million passengers every year. Serves remote Scottish destinations, as well as international ones.

'The heart of Scotland...'

Novelist Sir Walter Scott,
The Abbott *(1820)*

INTRODUCTION

Edinbroo! 'Auld Reekie',[1] 'Quite enchanting!',[2] 'The Athens of the North',[3] 'Scotia's darling seat',[4] 'World Festival City' (modest, huh?)[5] or even a 'mad god's dream'[6] of architectural splendour – Edinburgh has been all things to all men (and women). Proud, prosperous and famously prim – at least, if contrasted with warmer-hearted Glasgow or the wilder Highlands and Islands – it's been Scotland's capital for over 500 years, and is still the most powerful Scottish

1. Poet Robert Fergusson (1773). 2. Queen Victoria, quoting Prince Albert (1842). 3. artist Hugh William Williams (c 1820). 4. poet Robert Burns (1786). 5. the Scottish Government (2013). 6. poet Hugh MacDairmid (1978)

city today. It was not always so. For centuries, Edinburgh was small and insignificant. It was not even Scotland's chief town. For a long while, it belonged to an English kingdom. Once, there were rumours that it had been founded by an English, not Scottish, king.

Yet, as the years rolled by, Edinburgh grew – and how. First soldiers, then monks and friars, then market-traders, wool and hide merchants, butchers and bakers, brewers, innkeepers, shady entertainers, fishermen, ship-builders, kings, lawyers, parliaments and preachers, all came to live in the cramped and beguiling Old Town.

Once Edinburgh became Scotland's capital around 1437, they were followed by people who made or imported fine, costly things for the rich to enjoy: poems and printed books, French silk, lace and red wine, German swords, Eastern spices, Baltic furs, Italian jewels and oil-paintings. Until the Union of 1707 began to lure Edinburgh's movers and shakers south of the Border to the royal court and parliament of London, the city was the centre of power, politics, law and culture for the whole of

Scotland, with close ties to many other great European cities, from Scandinavia to southern France. A second age, perhaps of even greater glory, began around 1750, when thinkers, writers and scientists made Edinburgh their home – and moved to inhabit its most suitably rational, elegant New Town quarter.

Famous – infamous, even – for its year-round bracing climate, Edinburgh is the place where 'the delicate die early', according to its most famous invalid, novelist Robert Louis Stevenson (*Treasure Island*, *Kidnapped*), although he classed himself as a survivor. It's certainly a place where countless lives have been lost to plots and plague and poverty, to drink and desperation. Where proud and principled men have died for their beliefs or their politics, where scheming women have been burnt as witches, and where a foolish queen lost her crown for the love of a handsome rogue. Where a doomed, romantic rebel prince enjoyed a fleeting taste of glory; where schoolboys shot a magistrate (see page 100), a young student was hanged for atheism, and the last woman to be accused of black magic in Britain practised her dark arts.

Edinburgh has been the home of world-changing thinkers, pioneer doctors, remarkably inventive criminals – and a new, improved guillotine to get rid of them. It inspired the sinister story of 'Jekyll and Hyde' and the even more sordid *Trainspotting*. Yes, the Harry Potter books were written there, too, and Hogwarts School buildings perhaps owe some of their appearance to the extravagant exterior of public school Fettes College (founded 1870). It was the place where the *Encyclopaedia Britannica* was first compiled, where Britain's first digestive biscuits were made – and (however much this might offend the good citizens of St Andrews) the site of the world's earliest golf club.

Today, Edinburgh is still stalked by memories, haunted by ghosts. It's a place of 'dark nights and candlelight, and intellect'.[7] A place where 'something from the past just comes and stares into my soul.'[8] The city also, of course, tries very hard to be modern. Not an easy feat for a World Heritage Site, with the largest proportion of protected buildings in any UK town, and

7. *novelist Robert Louis Stevenson (1903).* 8. *novelist Alexander MacCall Smith (2004);*

some of the grandest historic cityscapes in the whole of Europe…

Since 1999, Scotland's parliament has once again met in the city, and is now housed in a vastly expensive and controversial new building. Not to be outdone, Edinburgh's city government has made (and cut back) its own ambitious budget-busting plans, for trams. Citizens lament the – hopefully temporary – decline of the traditional banking and finance industries after the economic crisis of 2008; until very recently, one in every four city workers was employed in the finance industry or businesses related to it.

However, all are united in praise of Edinburgh University, officially a 'world leader' not only in the latest medical and veterinary research, but also in future-forward informatics. Like other big cities, Edinburgh has some serious social deprivation, with crime, drug problems, poor housing, homelessness and unemployment. Until recently, the southern suburb of Craigmillar was classified as the fourth most deprived area in Scotland (out of over 1,200).

In spite of its troubles, Edinburgh remains Scotland's top tourist destination, second only to London in the UK for the number of visitors (13 million) each year. At Festival time, in the summer, they swarm the streets and almost double the city's population (outside festival times, approaching 500,000). The streets are crowded, too, for the strange but picturesque institution of the Edinburgh Tattoo, and at Hogmanay, for frosty torchlight processions and a magnificent fireworks display.

So, Edinburgh! Ancient and modern. Gracious and grimy. Haunt of philosophers, shopkeepers, writers and artists, tourists and students, lawyers and criminals, the proud, the famous and the poor. With a dramatic past, a current Pledge to build 'a Cooperative Capital'[9](yes really), and – just perhaps – the prospect of fresh greatness and glory. How and why? Because, in 2014, if certain politicians have their way, Edinburgh might once again become the capital of an independent nation.

9. *Edinburgh City Council (2013).*

Yes, another one...

On his first visit to Edinburgh, English scholar and author Dr Samuel Johnson remarked that it was 'a city too well known to admit description'.

Dr Johnson was one of the greatest minds of his age, but his wise words have passed unheeded. Since 1775, when his *A Journey to the Western Islands of Scotland* was first published, a positive *plype* or *gandiegow* (Scots: downpour) of poems, pamphlets, prints, plays, photos, and, of course, books big and small, has attempted to portray 'Fair Edina'.

Readers, here is yet another modest contribution. Enjoy!

first, some facts and figures – Edinburgh Today

What?

- **Capital city** of Scotland

- **Seat of the Scottish Parliament** and the Scottish Government (devolved national administration)

- **Run by:** City of Edinburgh Council; leader = the Lord Provost

- **Representation:** 5 UK MPs; 6 MSPs; 6 MEPs; 58 city councillors

- **Second largest** city in Scotland (Glasgow is bigger)

- **Number 5 among Scotland's richest districts.** Top of the table are East Renfrewshire and East Dumbartonshire – both have affluent commuter villages in pretty scenery close to Glasgow. They are followed by Stirling, an ancient royal burgh but now probably the most middle-class city in Scotland – and right next door to Andy Murray's home town of Dunblane. (Tennis is not a typical Scottish sport.) Ranked number four, Aberdeenshire's wealth is based on oil, oil, natural gas, oil, beef cattle, oil – and top-quality barley, used to make Scotch whisky.

- **Official residence** of HM the Queen in Scotland

- **Headquarters** of the national Church of Scotland

- **Home to four universities:** Edinburgh (ranked 21st in the world), Heriot Watt, Edinburgh Napier, and Queen Margaret. There are over 100 state-funded schools, and many ancient, exclusive, independent fee-paying ones. Approximately one city child in every four receives an independent education; that is three times the Scottish national average.

- **UNESCO World Heritage Site** (first listed 1995)

Where?

- **In** the eastern Central Lowlands of Scotland

- **On** the southern shore of the Firth (estuary) of the River Forth.

- **For** centuries, surrounded by Scotland's most kindly farming land – and some of its grimmest coal mines. Now the countryside close to the city is commuter territory, with just a few farms remaining.

- **Latitude:** 55.57° N (about the same as Moscow!)

- **Longitude:** 3.11° W (just east of Algiers!)

- **A long way** from London (332 miles/534 km as the crow flies; by road at least 405 miles/652 km). Amsterdam, at 410 miles/660 km distant, is not much further away.

- **Closest river:** The Water of Leith, a stream running from natural springs in the Pentland Hills (south of the city) past its southern and western borders, then entering the Firth of Forth at Leith.

- **Nearest port:** Leith (since 1920, part of Edinburgh) 4.00 km/2.5 miles away

- **Landscape:** Dramatic, majestic – and hilly (see pages 24–27).

- **City Area:** 264 square km/102 square miles; Larger Urban Zone (= city and surrounding settlements) 1,724 square km/666 square miles

- *Dreich* **and** *warie***?** (Scots: cold and depressing, hard and bleak) Well, yes, sometimes. Especially in winter, out-of-doors in Edinburgh is not a warm place to be. It's also very grey; in December and January, citizens are lucky to see the sun for 45 hours per month – that's barely an hour and a half every day. A *snell* (bitter) wind can whip around the castle crags and in between the tall old buildings. If it's from the southwest, which it usually is, it brings rain. If it's from the east, it carries in the *haar*, an east-coast speciality: thick grey sea-fog, which blots out Edinburgh's spectacular views and wets pedestrians to the bone.

But it's not all bad news on the climate front! Compared with other cities of the same latitude – or even further south – the Edinburgh climate is really very mild. Winter daytime temperatures rarely drop below freezing. Compared with the west coast of Scotland, Edinburgh is blissfully dry. (For seven months, February to August, rain does not fall on two days out of every three.) And, for visitors who hate the heat, it's good to know that the average summer temperature rarely exceeds 22° C/ 72° F. The highest ever recorded (in 1975) was a very modest 31.4° C /88.5° F. And, all through summer, there's often a cooling breeze.

It's usually said that the best time to visit Edinburgh is in April, May and June. Then, the city has its sunniest, driest days, and the late Scottish spring brings city trees into fresh green leaf and tempts flowers in city parks and gardens into early bloom. Even the lowering grey waters of the Firth of Forth glitter surprisingly clear and bright and blue.

Who?

- **Population (2011):** 495,360 (city); 778,000 (city plus surrounding Larger Urban Zone)

- **Population density:** 1,846 per square km

- **Edinburgh citizens** number just under 10 per cent of the total Scottish population. Statistically speaking, they are more youthful than the typical Scot. The median age of an Edinburgh citizen in 2011 was 35.1 years. Only in Glasgow is the average lower – and by just a tiny margin, at 34.9 years of age. This comparative youthfulness is partly the result of Edinburgh's prosperity, with high birthrates and low infant mortality, and partly the result of in-migration. Every year, large numbers of incomers, mostly students, temporary workers and well-educated young professional people, seek to make their homes in the city.

- **Edinburgh people** are also pretty long-lived, on the whole. But there are differences. A child born around 2005 in the pleasant, prosperous suburb of Fairmilehead can expect to live until he is 82; his sister might hope to survive until she is 89. But move the same boy and girl south to the deprived district of Craigmillar, and life expectancy falls sharply, to 70 for girls and only 65 for boys.

- **In term time,** students make up 20 per cent of the city population.

- **At Festival time**, Edinburgh welcomes another half a million visitors – or more.

- **All year round,** the city attracts tourists, from the UK and overseas. In 2010, there were 3.7 million recorded individual visits to Edinburgh. Visitors spent over one billion pounds sterling, and clocked up an astonishing total of 12.07 million 'bed-nights' in city tourist accommodation. That's an awful lot of sheets to change and wash for Edinburgh's hard-working chambermaids.

- **Edinburgh survives and thrives** not just by tourism. It is also one of Europe's most important financial centres, second only to London in the UK.

- **Parliamo Edinbroo?** The official language of Edinburgh (as decreed by the Scottish Government) is Scottish English; Scots is also spoken, and some Gaelic. Characteristically, Edinburgh Scots speakers tend to slur the 's' sound: think Sir Sean Connery. Otherwise, their light, mild accent, with typically Scottish rolled 'r's, guttural 'ch's and sharpened 'u' sounds, is generally very well regarded. In 2008, it came top of a preferred voices poll conducted by the BBC, scoring high marks for being both pleasant and prestigious, and symbolising a 'beautiful little nation with a long, proud history and oodles of art, music and other cultural capital.'[1]

Together with this civilised Edinburgh speech, there is, of course, the ineffable Morningside – a refined, not to say strangulated, accent affected by inhabitants of several genteel Edinburgh suburbs. How to describe? The favourite example is a cliché, but still true. To Morningside speakers, 'sex' are what the coal is delivered in. Enough said, maybe.

In perhaps a rather double-edged compliment, in 2009 Edinburgh was voted 'the top UK city to visit before you die'. BUT HOW did Edinburgh achieve such fame? WHEN? and WHY? Read on, and find out more!

1.   source: http://blog.scotweb.co.uk/journal/2008/2/21/do-scottish-accents-leave-you-shaken-or-stirred.html

Seven Hills

Like ancient Rome, Edinburgh was built on seven hills:

- **Castle Rock**
- **Calton Hill**
- **Corstorphine Hill**
- **Craiglockhart Hill**
- **Braid Hill**
- **Blackford Hill**
- **Arthur's Seat (including Crow Hill and Salisbury Crags)**

This happenstance gave the city great classical cachet among past scholars – and makes walking around it somewhat tiring, especially since many of the oldest, steepest, streets are paved with picturesque but uneven cobblestones.

- The most eminent, er, eminence, is of course **Castle Rock**, a craggy plug of tough black basalt rock spewed up by a fiery volcano around 350 million years ago. As we will see, there has been some kind of fortress here for 3,000 years.

- Close to modern Edinburgh's city centre, **Calton Hill** is home to the Scottish Government's administrative buildings and the Old Royal High School (founded in 1128, and one of the first-ever schools in Scotland). It is topped with historic monuments: the unfinished National Monument looks like a ruined Greek temple, the Nelson Monument, commemorating Britain's greatest naval commander, looks like an upturned telesope. The Dugald Stewart Monument honours an 18th-century philosopher (see page 139); the Robert Burns Monument shows Edinburgh's affection for Scotland's 'ploughman poet'. The Political Martyrs' Monument commemorates five Edinburgh men inspired by the French Revolution (1789) to campaign for 'power for the people'. They were convicted of sedition and transported to Australia in 1794 and 1795. The City Observatory, opened in 1898 on the site of earlier, smaller observatory buildings, was closed in 2009.

- Possibly the site of another ancient Celtic hill fort, in more recent centuries **Corstorphine Hill** housed a World War II radar station and a secret Cold War nuclear bunker. Today, it is home to Edinburgh Zoo, and its famous penguins and pandas.

- Prehistoric warriors, and the Romans, both left traces of their presence on **Craiglockhart Hill**. There is also a small, ruined medieval castle. In the 19th century, hospitals and a lunatic asylum were built on the hill; they later housed many soldiers suffering from shell-shock.

- **Braid Hill** was the site of important early discoveries by geologists. The rocks found there convinced them that the world was millions of years older than church scholars had calculated. There was a small medieval castle here and a famous 'Hermitage' (attractive country house, built 1785) in a steep wooded valley nearby.

- Like Braid Hill, **Blackford Hill** was studied by pioneer geologists. Swiss scholar Louis Agassiz (died 1873) found the first evidence here that glaciers had once covered Scotland. The Royal Observatory moved to Blackford Hill from Calton Hill in 1886, together with an important library of early books about astronomy.

- Another volcanic relic, the lumpy, crouching-lion-shaped ridge known as **Arthur's Seat**, towers 250.5 m (822 ft) above the city to the east. Described by Robert Louis Stevenson as 'a hill for magnitude, a mountain in virtue of its bold design', its name may commemorate an early Celtic ruler – perhaps even the famous King Arthur whose knights of the Round Table were later recorded in poems and songs.

  Less romantically, others point to the hill's strategic position, looming close to royal Holyrood Palace (and, today, the new Scottish Parliament), and suggest that its name is really Archers' Seat. Whatever its name means, Arthur's Seat has always been thought to have a romantic, holiday air:

  > Let me to Arthur's Seat pursue,
  > Where bonny pastures meet the view...
  > If fancy there would join the thrang
  > The desert hills and rocks amang,
  > To echoes we should lilt and play
  > And gie to mirth the lee-long day...

  Robert Fergusson, Auld Reekie, *1773*

Not wanting to miss out on any fun, by tradition, young Edinburgh girls crept out at dawn on Mayday morning to climb Arthur's Seat and bathe their faces in the beautifying dew:

> On May-day, in a fairy ring,
> We've seen them round St Anthon's spring,
> Frae grass the cauler [fresh] dew draps wring
>   To weet their een [eyes],
> And water clear as crystal spring
>   To synd [send] them clean . . .

Robert Fergusson, Callor Water, 1773

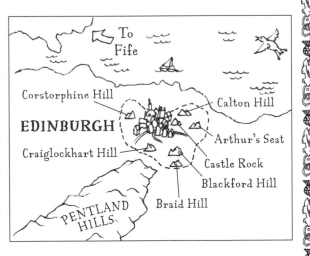

Edinburgh castle from the east

'A sad and solitary place, without
verdure, and, by reason of its vicinity
to the sea, unwholesome.'

*Margaret, Queen of Alexander III of
Scotland and daughter of Henry III
of England, writing to her father
in 1255, from Edinburgh Castle*

CHAPTER ONE

DIN EIDYN

(OR, THE FORT ON THE HILL)

O h dear. Poor Margaret! Married at 11 years old to a royal prince younger than herself, she was never happy in Scotland. Said to be 'a woman of great beauty, chastity and humility', she also had a hot temper. Early chroniclers reported how she (or her maid) playfully pushed a young squire who had displeased her into the River Tay, as he bent over to wash his hands in the water. He was swept away by the fast-flowing current, and drowned.

Margaret herself died aged 34, in 1275, and was buried in Dunfermline on the north bank of the Firth of Forth. At that time, Edinburgh was not yet Scotland's capital city; Dunfermline was where Scottish monarchs liked to hold their royal court (earlier kings chose Scone, near Perth; later kings preferred Stirling). And while kings still ran Scotland's government, the capital of their kingdom was wherever they happened to be.

But, however unimportant, sad, or solitary the place seemed to Queen Margaret, Edinburgh and its castle already had a long history by her time. Indeed, some of the earliest traces of human habitation in the whole of Scotland have been found there:

c. 13,000 BC The most recent Ice Age ends, and glaciers covering the north of the British Isles melt away. But, because much of the world's water is still locked up in polar ice-caps, sea levels are much lower than they are today. It's possible for bands of hunters and gatherers to splash across the shallow, dried-up North Sea, on foot or in dugout log canoes, from mainland Europe. They come from modern-day Germany, Denmark and the Netherlands to settle along the coast of eastern Scotland.

c. 8,500 BC Huge midden-heaps of discarded shells at Cramond, now a suburb to the northwest of Edinburgh, show that hunter-gatherers camped there, over and over again, to enjoy feasts of oysters and mussels from the southern shore of the Firth of Forth.

c. 8,000 BC Scotland's first house! (To be more precise, the oldest one found so far.) And it's near Edinburgh. In 2012, archaeologists working at Echline, South Queensferry, where a new road bridge is to be built across the Forth, make an exciting discovery. They find a shallow pit about 7 metres long, surrounded and criss-crossed by holes that once contained wooden poles that have long since rotted away. From these, they deduce that a large wooden shelter, like a conical tipi made of poles, once stood here. Inside, they find the remains of cosy hearth-fires and tasty, nutritious hazelnuts. Close by are 1,000 precisely made flint tools and arrowheads. These early Edinburghers hunted meat to eat, and probably wore fur.

c. 972–830 BC Castle Rock. Someone was lighting fires and cutting up animals where Edinburgh Castle now stands; the charcoal and bones remain, and can be scientifically dated. Archaeologists don't know who did this, but in the 1980s and 1990s, they also found fragments of Bronze Age pottery (in Scotland, bronze-working technology continued until 71–84 AD), and a stone saddle-quern, used for grinding grain – perhaps to make porridge or bannocks (cakes cooked on a hot, flat surface). Although meagre, this evidence suggests that people were now living permanently not far from Castle Rock; grain-growers do not usually move far from the crops they have planted.

c. 1st to 3rd centuries AD By now, the evidence is clear. There are at least two typical 'Celtic' Iron Age roundhouses on flat land at the top of Castle Rock, with wooden walls, turf roofs, cobble and flagstone floors and neat stone boxes where hearth fires were kept burning. These homes were built directly on top of the earlier settlement; there is no sign of any break in occupation. There are also traces of defensive barriers nearby.

The people who lived here (or, at least, their leader) wore bronze jewellery and woollen clothes (archaeologists have found a spindle-whorl, used to twist yarn for weaving). They owned a lot of pottery, and used whetstones to sharpen tools – or weapons. This evidence suggests something much richer and grander than a simple farmstead: a Celtic chieftain's house or fort, probably.

There's no trace of farming here, but about a mile away, on the slopes of Arthur's Seat (see page 26), there are earthworks that suggest not only a farming village, but little cultivated fields, or gardens.

c. AD 100 By now, the Iron Age inhabitants of Edinburgh have met the Roman conquerors of Britain – fairly peacefully, it appears. Safe on top of Castle Rock, their possessions include rare luxuries: Roman glass and pottery, Roman-style metal brooches (used to pin cloaks), and even a Roman coin. The archaeologists who discovered these treasures say that the only other place nearby where comparable goodies have been found is the *ðun* (hill-fort) at Traprain Law, a steep, cone-shaped hill about 20 miles (32 km) south of Edinburgh – the stronghold of the Votadini.

33

Who were the Votadini?

Rich, powerful, sophisticated – they traded with faraway France – the Votadini were a confederation of Celtic tribes that controlled southeast Scotland at the time that Roman armies invaded in the 1st century BC. They:

- built hilltop forts, where they sheltered in times of danger, and which they also used for gatherings of warrior chiefs, and for religious ceremonies;

- were farmers, who grew grain, kept sheep and cattle, and surrounded their homesteads with defensive earthworks. They were expert metalworkers, and offered some of their finest creations as sacrifices to their gods;

- spoke a Celtic language, sometimes called 'Brythonic', which was distantly related to modern-day Welsh. (Further north in Scotland, people spoke a different Celtic tongue, the ancestor of modern Irish and Scottish Gaelic.)

- chose to make peace with invading Roman armies, rather than risk annihilation by confronting them, and became political 'clients' of the Roman rulers of north Britain.

We know about the Votadini because Roman writers Tacitus (a historian, d. AD 117) and Ptolemy (a geographer, d. AD 168) described them.

142 The Romans build forts at Cramond (now the outer northwest suburbs of Edinburgh) and Inveresk for their soldiers patrolling the Antonine Wall. Like the better-known Hadrian's Wall, the barrier built for Emperor Antonius Pius marked the far northwestern frontier of the Roman Empire, and defended Roman-occupied lands from barbarian attack. The fort is rebuilt in 209, to protect the Roman harbour at Cramond, on the Firth of Forth, but is abandoned within 50 years.

However, the Romans leave a wonderful statue there – the Cramond Lion. In fact a lioness, and a symbol of the might and pride of Rome, it shows her devouring a prisoner – presumably a recalcitrant Celtic warrior. Less confrontationally, the lioness also represents death, that must come to all. As a consoling thought, two snakes, symbols of everlasting life for the soul, twine themselves around the lioness. So all is not lost, for Celts or Romans.

c. 160 Roman geographer Ptolemy records that the Votadini live in 'a rocky place'. It's tempting to think he means Edinburgh's

Castle Rock, but we have no evidence to prove this.

c. 400 Roman armies leave the British Isles, for good. There's too much trouble in and around their homeland to waste time defending a distant frontier.

c. 500 Around this time, the Votadini seem to leave Traprain Law, and the hill-fort settlement on Edinburgh's Castle Rock becomes more important to them.

c. 603 or **617**, or **626** One of the earliest surviving Welsh poems, by the bard Aneurin, describes how the army of the Gododdin (the later Welsh version of the name Votadini), from a place called Din Eidyn, attacked the king of the Anglian people at Catterick in Yorkshire – and, alas, was annihilated.

In Celtic languages, *Din Eidyn* means either 'the fort on the hill slope' or 'the stronghold of Eidyn'. In this context, where else can that be but Castle Hill in Edinburgh?

For a year before the battle, the bard tells how the leader of the Gododdin, King Mynyddog Mwynfawr (Mynyddog the Wealthy), feasted lesser chieftains in his great hall at Din Eidyn. The warriors reclined on soft, white sheeps' fleeces, drank deeply, sang, boasted – and probably fathered children on complaisant serving girls. Perhaps they staggered outside, as well, to practice their fighting skills. They knew that if they failed in combat their lives would soon be over.

And, despite their bravery, that was indeed so. Aneurin boasts:

> 'Bloodstained were their swords,
> May their spears never be clean...'

But then truth forces him to admit:

> 'None escaped but three,
> through brave deeds of combat ...'

638 Just a few years later, the Iona Chronicle, written on a remote island on the far western side of Scotland, reports that an unnamed Anglian King (perhaps King Oswald) has taken control of all the Votadini/Goddodin lands. From its original home in Northumberland, Oswald's Anglian kingdom now controls a vast (and rich) area, from Scotland's River Tay to England's Humberside – including Edinburgh.

A name for a city

In the past, historians used to say that the Anglian king Edwin of Northumbria (died 633), gave his name to Edinburgh ('Edwinesborough'). Or that the city was named after a legendary British king, Ebraucus. Clearly a very busy man, Ebraucus allegedly had 20 wives and 50 children, and founded the cities of York and Dumbarton, too...

It is not so. While *burgh* is undoubtedly an Old English word, meaning 'fortified town', Edinburgh's Celtic name, Din Eidyn (the fortress on the hill slope) existed long before King Edwin came to power. So Edinburgh is mixed – part Celtic, part Old English. Just like the Scots language (see page 23) that is still spoken there.

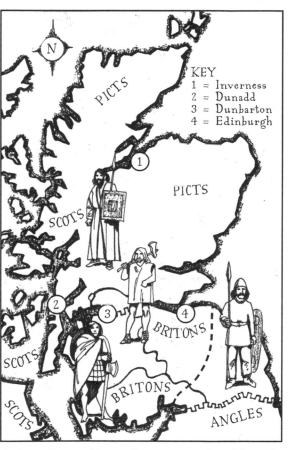

KEY
1 = Inverness
2 = Dunadd
3 = Dunbarton
4 = Edinburgh

PICTS

PICTS

SCOTS

SCOTS

SCOTS

BRITONS

BRITONS

ANGLES

The four Kingdoms in Scotland
around AD 600.

One Land, four Peoples

At the time (around 638) King Oswald conquered Edinburgh, Scotland was not yet a united nation. Instead, it was divided between four rival peoples:

- Picts ruled the North and East from their stronghold at Inverness.

- Scots ruled the far West; their royal centre was at Dunadd.

- Britons ruled Strathclyde, a kingdom in south-west Scotland. They were based in Dun Breatainn (the Fort of the Britons, now Dumbarton, near Glasgow).

- Other Britons (the Gododdin/Votadini) lived in and around Edinburgh.

Oswald's mighty kingdom of Northumbria was home to Britons, as well, but also to Anglian settlers, who arrived from what is now Germany, the Netherlands, and perhaps southern Denmark. Oswald himself was descended from Anglian and Saxon kings and princesses. He was killed in battle in AD 642, fighting against warrior-kings in East Anglia.

Tribes, warlords and kings

The Picts, Scots and Britons in Scotland all spoke related, Celtic languages (the ancestors of modern Gaelic and Welsh), and shared many traditions. They were farmers, hunters, and skilled craft-workers. They loved music and poetry, fine clothes and feasting. They admired bravery and fighting skills. Often, their rival tribes fought each other. But slowly, over the centuries, a few ruling families, led by powerful warlords, joined the warring tribes together.

By the early 9th century, the Pictish and Scottish kingdoms were ruled by the same powerful dynasty. Although the two kingdoms were not yet joined together, they could organise a united attack:

840 Pictish/Scottish king Cinaed mac Ailpin (Kenneth MacAlpine) raids Northumbria, burning Dunbar and possibly Edinburgh, too.

854 Just possibly, the holy hermit Cuthbert of Lindisfarne, patron saint of the Angles of Northumbria, preaches at Edinburgh.

Later traditions also say that he founded the first Christian church there. But there is no evidence.

960 The Chronicle of the Kings of Alba (Scotland, i.e. united Picts and Scots) records that the 'oppidum [fortress or fortified town] Eden . . . was evacuated, and abandoned to the Scots until the present day'. The king of Scotland at that time was Indulf (reigned 954–962); the kings who followed him kept hold of Din Eidyn, in spite of English counterattacks.

973 According to legend, King Edgar the Peaceful, who ruled most of England, commanded that six lesser British kings should row him in his royal boat on the River Dee, near Chester. These kings included Kenneth II of Scotland; in return for this act of submission, Edgar accpted Kenneth's right to rule the land around Edinburgh.

1020 King Malcolm defeats the Northumbrians at the Battle of Carham just south of the River Tweed. The Scots now control Edinburgh and land to the south, as far as the border with England.

1074 Malcolm II's son, Scottish king Malcolm III Canmore ('Big Chief'), rebuilds the fortress at Edinburgh. His royal court is at Dunfermline, on the north shore of the Firth of Forth, but he also spends time in Edinburgh, presumably because of the fort's strategic and military importance. And, although still made of wood, Malcolm's fort now has royal living quarters as well. We know this because…

1093 Queen Margaret (a different one from the unhappy lassie described on page 29), saintly wife of Malcolm III, dies in her chamber in the royal castle at 'the fort on the hill of Agned'. (According to early writers, Agned was another name for Edinburgh.)

Place of Peace, or War?

Today, tourists are often told that a small stone structure, part of Edinburgh Castle, is the oldest building in Edinburgh. Now known as 'St Margaret's Chapel', this small, peaceful chamber is still used as a place of worship. Queen Margaret was famous for her piety and good deeds, and protected the church in Scotland. She was made a saint, by the Pope, in 1250. But alas, she did not say her prayers at the chapel now named after her. Almost certainly, she never saw it. The building known today as St Margaret's Chapel dates from maybe 100 years after she died.

It is very possible that Margaret's son, Scotland's King David I, paid for a chapel to be built at Edinburgh fort/castle as a memorial to his mother. But it may not be the building that we see now. In fact, some archaeologists think that the stone walls of 'St Margaret's Chapel' are more likely to be part of Malcolm III's strong new castle keep.

Edinburgh Castle

One o'clock Gun

Mons Meg

KEY

1 New Barracks
2 Butt's Battery
3 Hospital
4 St. Margaret's Chapel
5 Portcullis Gate
6 Half Moon Battery
7 The Esplanade
8 Vaults
9 Military Prison
10 Great Hall
11 Governor's House
12 Water Tank
13 Royal Palace
14 Gatehouse
15 Foog's Gate
16 Scottish National War Memorial

Ground Plan

And so we see that, by around 1200, the hill-fort is turning into a royal castle, or perhaps has already become one. And where there are kings and queens, there will be courtiers and bodyguards and maidservants and manservants and cooks and cleaners and nurses and tutors and priests and entertainers – to say nothing of a troop or two of soldiers with knights on horseback, and saddle-makers and armourers, and washerwomen and sweepers and grooms. And, of course, royal messengers and foreign ambassadors and other important guests.

All these people will need food and clothes and somewhere to sleep (and so will their horses). The castle itself will need constant repairs. And so, if, outside the fort or castle walls, there was not already a settlement of people ready and willing to provide supplies, there very soon would be...

'The houses stand more crowded than
in any other town in Europe.'

Early visitor to Edinburgh

CHAPTER TWO

WOOL, HIDES, FISH AND WAR

fish is not glamorous, prestigious or dignified. It never has been, and probably never will be. And yet it played an important part in Edinburgh's rise to greatness — along with other smelly, bulky, basic products: sheeps' wool, cattle-hides, coal and, later, linen. They were the main commodities produced in fields and farms and seas close to Edinburgh, processed by its townsfolk, and sold in its booths (shops) and marketplaces.

No-one knows precisely when town life at Edinburgh began. The Romans built no towns in Scotland, and the warlike years before

Scottish kings took control of the hill-fort at Edinburgh, around AD 960, do not seem particularly promising for the development of peaceful trade. But maybe a few enterprising merchants settled close to the Castle Rock hill-fort, offering to provide essential foodstuffs for kings and warriors sheltering there, or, more likely, being ordered to bring a tribute of their best produce to feed visiting royalty and their hungry retinues.

It's also very possible that, protected by Malcolm III's wooden castle of around 1080 (see page 43) and by later, stronger, stone castle walls, the little commercial community of Edinburgh slowly grew and prospered, getting busier, more crowded, and more dirty and smelly, year by year. Medieval kings liked towns; their people paid taxes.

Crag~and~tail

Where was this trading town built? Not on Castle Rock itself, but on stones and soil deposited by retreating glaciers (around 110,000–10,000 years ago), immediately to the east. As the glaciers passed Castle Rock (a volcanic plug of hard, craggy basalt), its sheer bulk and solidity forced the ice to divide. The softer material carried by the glaciers was dropped behind the rock as a narrow ridge, for around a mile on its eastward side, creating what geologists call a typical 'crag-and-tail' formation.

A 16th-century traveller described Edinburgh's layout very well:

'...the City riseth higher and higher towards the West, and consists especially of one broad and very faire street [today, known as the Royal Mile] (which is the greatest part and sole ornament thereof), the rest of the side streetes and allies being of poore building and inhabited with very poore people, and this length, from the East to the West is about a mile, whereas the bredth of the City from the

North to the South is narrow, and cannot be
halfe a mile. At the farthest end towards the
West, is a very strong Castle...'

Fynes Moryson, Itinerary, *Part i, Book iii.*
Chap. 5. 1598

With its 'spine' of a long High Street, and its
numerous 'ribs' of narrow side-streets (known
as *wynds*), local people, clearly still with fish on
their minds, said that Edinburgh's street-plan
looked just like a 'gutted haddie' (haddock).

A church for the community

The first document to mention Edinburgh
town, rather than its royal castle, dates
from 1124 (or perhaps 1127). It records the
existence of 'the church of the . . . burgh of
Edin'. A church implies a settled, thriving
community, with enough money to support
at least one priest and maintain a building
for worship. The Edinburgh church was
dedicated to St Giles – a vegetarian, forest-
dwelling hermit with a special fondness for
red deer. That seems appropriate for Scotland,
which still harboured bears, wolves, lynx and

beavers as well as countless deer, at the time. The choice of patron saint suggests that the land around Edinburgh was still very rural. It may just possibly have links with the story of the Sacred Stag of Holyrood (see page 62). Or it may reflect nothing more than ecclesiastical fashion. In many parts of Europe, St Giles was honoured as the protector of people with physical and mental disabilities, and prayed to by women hoping for children, or anyone suffering from the plague.

Probably the town church stood on the same site as today's Edinburgh High Kirk (also, but erroneously, known as 'St Giles Cathedral') – to the east of the Castle, about 350 metres along the narrow ridge that forms the High Street section of the Royal Mile.

By Royal Appointment

Around the same time as we hear of the townspeople's church, King David I of Scotland granted Edinburgh a royal charter in 1125. Why did he do this, and what did it mean? King David was a moderniser, keen to copy 'civilised' institutions from more developed countries such as England and France, and introduce them to Scotland. These novelties included burgh charters – grants of special status by kings (or by other locally important people), confirmed in a written document validated with impressive wax seals bearing royal or noble portraits.

The grant of a burgh charter was a two-way deal, promoting the wealth of a monarch's kingdom – and giving burgh inhabitants the right to govern themselves, control local businesses, appoint magistrates (local judges) and generally manage their own affairs. Royal burghs like Edinburgh also had a very profitable monopoly on overseas trade. By 1162, Scottish kings felt confident enough about Edinburgh's future to make it the base for their chief royal representative in the region: the sheriff of Lothian. Land within the royal burgh was allocated to local merchants and craftsmen. The first merchants each occupied a *toft*, a long, narrow strip of land stretching back from a narrow frontage on the High Street. (This is the origin of the city's 'gutted haddie' street layout.) Once a toft had been granted, the lucky merchant had to build a house on the High Street within a year and a day, or forfeit his toft. He usually enclosed the land behind his house, as well, and if his business prospered, built workshops and warehouses there, too. Later, merchants filled these tofts with *closes* and houses. At the far end of the toft, he added a gate leading to a back lane, encircling the whole town settlement.

In 1329, King Robert I (aka war-hero Robert the Bruce) granted Edinburgh a second charter, giving it control over the nearby seaport of Leith. Goods landed there could only be sold in Edinburgh, and by Edinburgh merchants. The Leith inhabitants were angry – but powerless. Soon afterwards, in 1333, export trade through Leith received a tremendous boost, when English armies captured Berwick-on-Tweed, the leading port in southeast Scotland. All Berwick's Scottish export trade, mostly in hides and leather, was re-routed through Leith, and Edinburgh merchants profited. By the 1440s, Edinburgh/Leith was also handling almost half of all Scotland's wool exports. In 1449, Edinburgh merchants exported over 40,000 sheepskins and 24,000 hides.

By the 1360s, visitors to Edinburgh counted around 400 dwellings in the burgh; French chronicler Jean Froissart called it 'the Paris of Scotland'. In 1437, Scottish king James III declared that Edinburgh was 'the principal burgh in our kingdom' – in effect, Scotland's capital. By the early 1500s, this royal approval was reflected in the amount of tax that Edinburgh townsfolk had to pay: around one-quarter of the national total. And tolls on Edinburgh's import–export trade contributed one-half of all Scotland's customs revenues.

This economic growth was helped by improved communications: around 1072, saintly Queen Margaret, wife of Malcolm III, gave money to set up a new ferry service across the Firth of Forth. Margaret's aim was to help pilgrims making their pious way to St Andrews, further north, in Fife, but her ferry also made life easier for merchants, lawyers, royal officials – and royalty – travelling to and from Edinburgh. However, one ill-advised crossing at Queensferry led to a Scottish constitutional crisis...

ferry folly

The year was 1296. It was, as they say, a dark and stormy night. King Alexander III had spent a busy few days, carousing with friends in Edinburgh Castle to celebrate his second marriage, and holding meetings with his advisors, who were presumably based there. But now, business finished, he was keen to get back to Dunfermline, where his new wife was waiting.

The weather was truly awful; the advisors begged Alexander to stay. But he refused. He was always impetuous, and (as Edinburgh folk might say) always a great man for the ladies: 'He used never to forbear on account of season nor storm, nor for perils of flood or rocky cliffs, but would visit none too creditably nuns or matrons, virgins or widows as the fancy seized him, sometimes in disguise...' Alexander was also a widower; all his children had died. He desperately needed an heir, and his new wife was young and pretty. He managed the Queensferry crossing, but then got lost in the storm. He was found, dead, at daylight next morning at the foot of a steep rocky slope. Alexander's only heir was a three-year-old half-Scottish, half-Scandinavian princess, 'the Maid of Norway'. And she died on the voyage to Scotland, in 1290.

Later legends told how Alexander should have taken more care. A frightful apparition, half skeleton, half rotting flesh, had appeared at his wedding feast – a traditional death warning.

Later royal patronage helped Edinburgh by providing improved commercial facilities. In 1364, King David II gave land to the citizens, so they could build a new *tron* (public balance), for weighing goods reliably and combating fraud. Four years later, King Robert II granted more land, for a tolbooth. This became a meeting house for burgh leaders, a counting-house for paying tolls and taxes, and, soon after, a ghastly prison.

The Heart of Midlothian

That was the romantic name given to a very nasty place – the Edinburgh Tolbooth and its condemned cell (an iron cage where prisoners waiting for execution were confined). Now, the Old Tolbooth is long gone (it was demolished in 1817) and the site is marked by a heart-shaped pattern of coloured granite stones set into the cobbled street.

Today, it's a rather unpleasant custom to spit on the heart as you pass by. This is said to be in memory of prisoners released from captivity, who spat at the Tolbooth to show their disgust as they walked through its door to freedom. And very disgusting it was. Edinburgh historian Hugh Arnot, visiting the Tolbooth in 1778, reported that: 'such an incredible stench assailed us, from the stagnant and putrid air, as utterly to overpower us…'

Even more important, the Edinburgh Tolbooth began to be used as a place for assemblies of the Scottish Parliament. Composed of representatives of Scotland's Three Estates (clergy, nobles and royal townsfolk – poor peasants didn't get a look-in), parliaments were originally summoned to advise and support Scottish kings, and then to sanction demands for potentially unpopular taxes. At first, they met wherever the king was – in big churches, at royal castles, at historic open-air sites, and more than once, close to the field of battle. By the early 15th century, the Blackfriars Church at Scone, near Perth, was a favourite meeting place. But after hapless King James I was assassinated there, the Scottish Parliament moved to Edinburgh for safety, and the city became its main home until 1707. Already, Edinburgh Castle was being used to house royal officials responsible for royal accounts and record-keeping. The arrival of the Parliament made Edinburgh, without doubt, Scotland's premier city.

Edinburgh 'passis them all'

'On the south side of Forth lyis Louthiane … maist plentuus ground of Scotland. In it ar mony abbayis, castellis, and townis… bot Edinburgh passis thaim all, baith in polese, reputation, wisdome, and riches.'

Hector Boece [say Boyce] (translated from Latin into Scots by John Bellenden), Chronicles of Scotland, 1536

[lyis = lies; Louthiane = Lothian; an ancient region of Scotland, said to be called after semi-legendary King Loth of the Pictish people. The same name is still used for the area around Edinburgh today.
maist plentuus = most rich and productive; passis = surpasses; baith = both; polese = policy = government

From 1532, the Court of Session, one of the highest in the land, also met in Edinburgh; by 1485, at least one professional notary was living there, and presumably earning his income by drawing up business deals and recording commercial transactions. The first printing press in Scotland, run by Walter Chapman and Andrew Myllar of Edinburgh, was granted a royal licence by James IV in 1507. By the same date, there were 15 separate, specialised markets along the High Street.

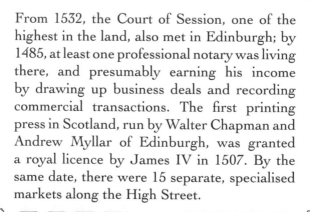

Skilled Edinburgh workers were also organising themselves into trade associations, or guilds. Even today, the Edinburgh Trades treasure an ancient banner, known as the Blue Blanket. According to tradition, this was presented to them by James III in 1482. Since then, it has served as a rallying point whenever they felt their collective values (however defined) to be threatened.

By the 1530s, there were fourteen – or maybe fifteen – different craftsmen's guilds in Edinburgh: surgeons, goldsmiths, skinners, furriers, hammermen, wrights (carpenters) and masons, tailors, baxters (bakers), fleshers (butchers), bonnetmakers and dyers, cordiners (leather-workers), websters (weavers), waulkers (cloth-finishers), and candlemakers. And, although not recognised as guilds, there were also reckoned to be 288 alewives (brewers) in the city, together with 367 merchants. Like other cities throughout Europe, Edinburgh was visited by outbreaks of plague – the worst were in 1568, 1584–1588 and 1645. Even so, because of constant migration into the city, the population doubled between 1550 and 1625, and tripled by 1650.

Names and places

The early history of Edinburgh's trade is still recorded in city street-names. Here are just a few:

Bread Street
Candlemaker Row
Coal Hill
Convening Court (where all the trade guilds/associations convened, or met)
Cowfeeder Row
Cowgate (the street along which cows – kept for milk, butter and cheese – were driven out of the city to pasture. See illustration on next page.)
Hardwell Close (Edinburgh did not have a plentiful natural water supply. Most water came from deep wells; there was no running water until 1672, when it was piped to public drinking fountains from Coniston Springs.)
Fishmarket Close (of course)
Grassmarket (where hay was sold); also **Haymarket** (outside the city)
Hammermen's Close
Horse Wynd (site of the royal stables), also **Kings' Stables**
Jock's Lodge (where a town beggar built a shack)
Lady Wynd (from a chapel to Our Lady, the Virgin Mary)
Lawnmarket (where lawn – smooth linen or woollen cloth – was sold)
Market Street
Merchant Street
Middle Baxters' (Bakers') Close
Shoemakers' Close

Just outside the city:

Bakehouse Close (city leaders preferred anyone working with fire, such as bakers, to live outside the city. Close-packed city houses, made of wood and thatched with dried grass or heather, were dangerously inflammable.)

Damside (beside the mill dam across the Water of Leith; watermills ground grain to make flour.)

Fishwives' Causey (raised roadway, leading to the fishing port of Musselburgh, on the coast)

Bowling Green Close (think Sir Francis Drake...)

High Riggs (high ridges of land, where crops were grown)

Greenside (a natural level open space, by the road to Leith, used to hold races, tournaments etc.)

Potterrow (where potters worked in clay, and fired their kilns)

Tanfield (where tanners and other hide-workers carried out their messy, dirty, smelly business. Like potters and bakers, they were not welcome inside the city.)

Slaughter Road

Old houses in the Cowgate

Although often criticised as savage and barbaric by its English neighbours, medieval Scotland had a great deal of time for religion. Just a few years after he granted a royal charter to Edinburgh, King David I of Scotland founded Holyrood Abbey. It was sited on low-lying pastureland at the end of the 'tail' of earth trailing eastwards from Edinburgh's Castle Rock, in the shadow of Arthur's Seat.

According to tradition, David received the call to establish his Abbey in a direct – and dangerous – way. In 1228, while staying at Edinburgh Castle, he went hunting on the slopes of Arthur's Seat. It was a Sunday, the Christian holy day, and he should have been at his prayers rather than enjoying rest and recreation. As David galloped along, he saw a huge and beautiful stag, and was determined to kill it. He hurled his spear at the beast; it was wounded, but still standing. Closing in for the kill, King David found himself unhorsed, on the ground, in mortal danger. Then he saw that his sword had became entangled in the stag's antlers, and now appeared as a cross in front of his eyes. Who knows how, but David survived. In gratitude, he founded Holy Rood

– the monastery of the holy cross. A whole new royal burgh (named Canongate) developed around it, and along the street leading up to the eastern limits of Edinburgh.

Not to be outdone, later kings, queens and townsfolk gave money to support religious orders in Edinburgh: Blackfriars, Greyfriars, Carmelites, religious hospitals and hospices, a leper sanctuary, at least two convents of nuns – plus a hermit (Holy Bernard) who lived in a cave.

Buried treasures

In 2012, the history world was fascinated by the discovery of the bones of England's King Richard III under a supermarket car-park. Not to be outdone, Edinburgh has its own spectacular discovery: the tomb of a noble knight plus 15 other medieval people – in a car park, too. The graves are interesting in themselves: the knight's tomb is covered by a sandstone slab carved with a Crusader cross and ornate sword. But they have also provided exciting new information – the site of the 'lost' Blackfriars church, which was founded in 1230 by King Alexander II (ruled 1214–1249) and destroyed during the Protestant Reformation in 1559.

Meanwhile, in the castle...

Remarkably, Edinburgh achieved its economic growth and political success in wild and war-torn times. Although Scots liked to think that its castle-on-a-crag was impregnable, this was not so. In the wars that raged between around 1100 and 1550, Edinburgh castle was captured, pulled down, rebuilt and captured, again and again.

1107 Like his mother, Queen Margaret (see page 43), Prince Edgar of Scotland died in the castle – probably newly rebuilt, of wood, on the orders of his brother, King David I.

1153–1165 Frail, pious King Malcolm IV 'the Maiden' makes Edinburgh Castle his home.

1174 Rough, red-headed King William I, 'the Lion', is captured in battle by the English and forced to hand over Edinburgh Castle to them. English troops occupy it for 12 years, until William agrees to marry a Norman princess, chosen for him (for political reasons) by King Henry II of England. She produces four children in less than 8 years – and then dies.

c. 1290 There are rival candidates for the Scottish throne. King Edward I of England claims the right to choose one. He stays at Edinburgh Castle and demands homage from reluctant Scottish nobles.

1296 England's Edward I – now nicknamed 'the Hammer of the Scots' – takes advantage of Scotland's political uncertainty and invades. He besieges Edinburgh Castle, which surrenders after 3 days. He installs a garrison of over 300 soldiers and some top military engineers. He also plunders the holy relics that are stored there – national treasures (including the crown) and the ancient, mystical Stone of Destiny – and takes them to England.

The Stone of Destiny heads for England

The Stone of Destiny

It's big and heavy (around 152 kg), it's chipped and battered, it's nothing much to look at, and it may be a fake. Even so, the Stone of Scone, also known as the Stone of Destiny, holds a special place in the hearts of most Scots men and women.

According to legend, the Stone was the pillow of Hebrew patriarch Jacob. He slept on it and saw angels climbing up and down to heaven. Magically, it flew to Scotland. Then Scottish kings – possibly even the murderous MacBeth – sat on it to be crowned.

From 1296, the Stone of Destiny 'lived' in England. Or did it? In 2008, Scottish National Party politician Alex Salmond claimed that medieval monks had palmed King Edward off with a fake, and hidden the real Stone somewhere in Scotland.

Real or false, a Stone remained in London's Westminster Abbey until 1950, when Scottish students 'kidnapped' it. In 1996, it was officially returned to Scotland, and is now on display in Edinburgh Castle.

1307 Edward I dies, and the Scots breathe a big sigh of relief. But the English still hold Edinburgh Castle.

1314 Scottish noble Thomas Randolph, earl of Moray, leads a party of 30 hand-picked men to climb up the cliffs and into the castle. They drive the English out, but then...

1315 ...on the orders of Scotland's King Robert the Bruce I, Edinburgh Castle is pulled down, to stop the English occupying it again.

1333 England's King Edward II invades; two years later (1335), his armies capture the ruins of Edinburgh Castle, in one assault sheltering behind a wall of slaughtered warhorses. Later, they rebuild it.

1341 In a Trojan-horse-style trick, Scots led by William Douglas disguise themselves as Edinburgh merchants and get inside the castle. They open the gates to let the Scots army in; the English garrison is massacred.

1357 Peace with England. Scotland's King David II rebuilds the castle again, adding a tall stone tower-house, for accommodation and shelter.

1370s After David's death, King Robert II of Scotland continues to rebuild the castle.

1400 England's King Henry IV besieges the castle, but is forced to retreat, because of lack of supplies.

c. 1440s Extensive rebuilding at the castle, including beginnings of a separate 'palace block' (purpose-built royal living accommodation).

1440 The 'Black Dinner':

> Hush ye, hush ye,
> Dinna fret ye,
> The Black Douglas
> Will nae get ye.

Well over 600 years after the 'Black[1] Douglas' died, the author remembers her father repeating this rather scary lullaby. What's it about? James Douglas, Lord of Douglas (died 1330) was a formidable warlord. He

---

1. the nickname came from his black hair

helped make the Douglas family the strongest in Lowland Scotland; they were sometimes allies, but more often rivals, of the ruling Steward dynasty. In 1440, Stewart King James II was just 10 years old. William, 6th Lord of Douglas, was about 5 years older.

The king's guardians feared that the Douglas clan might try to replace James with William. And William's uncle, greedy James the Gross, wanted to replace William as Douglas clan chief. So they plotted together and invited William and his younger brother to a feast in Edinburgh Castle. At the end, they served up a huge black bull's head on a platter – a traditional sign of death. William and his brother were taken outside and beheaded; young King James was powerless to help them.

> Edinburgh castle, town and tower,
> God grant you sink for sin!
> And that even for the black dinner
> Earl Douglas got therein.

Traditional rhyme, spelling modernised

1457 An unusual present, perhaps, but King James II was pleased. He received a massive bombard (cannon), later nicknamed 'Mons Meg'. It was sent by Philip, Duke of Burgundy, to strengthen the defences of Edinburgh Castle, and to help the Scots fight the English.

This awesome weapon (it weighed over 6 tonnes and could fire 400 lb (180 kg) stone cannonballs at targets two miles away) together with the scientific interests of King James IV (died 1513), led to Edinburgh having the most important iron-foundry in Scotland. The wonderfully named 'master melter of the king's guns' cast cannon for use on Scottish royal warships and on the battlefield, as well as early hagbuts (hand-held guns).

Mons Meg remained popular with tourists for centuries:

'Amongst the many memorable things which I was shewed there [in Edinburgh], I noted especially a great peece of ordnance of iron... and it is so great within [inside], that it was told me that a childe was once gotten [conceived] there; but I, to make tryall crept into it, lying on my backe, and I am sure there was roome enough and spare for a greater than my selfe.'

John Taylor, The Pennyless Pilgrimage, *1618*

1464 New approach road built to the castle (still used today); more heavy artillery put in place, for defence.

1479 Duke of Albany is accused of plotting against his brother, King James III, and imprisoned in the castle. He gets his guards drunk (or drugged) and escapes by making a daring descent from a castle window.

1482 Albany leads an army to try to overthrow James III. For safety, James shuts himself away inside the castle, and becomes a prisoner.

1528 James IV – who was said to have liked 'the bigging [building] of palaces' gives orders to build a new royal residence, Holyrood House; the canons (priests living as monks) are moved out of their living quarters, although the monastery church remains. From now on

Edinburgh Castle is used less often as royal lodgings – although in 1566 Mary Queen of Scots is taken there to give birth to her only son, James VI and I. She is lodged in a tiny room. Later visitors are shocked: 'It would scarcely be occupied, save under protest, by a housemaid in our days…'

But, as we will see in Chapter 3, all that is another story.

The northwest tower of Holyrood
Palace, built for Scotland's King
James V between 1528 and 1536.

Pour lui j'ai hazardé grandeur et
  conscience,
Pour lui tous mes parents j'ai quittés, et
  amis
Et tous autres respects sont a part mis.
Brief, de vous seul je cherche l'alliance.

For him I have risked rank and
  conscience,
For him I have left my family and
  friends
And all other thoughts I have put aside.
In short, I seek your love alone.

*From a poem describing Mary Queen of
Scots's feelings for James Hepburn, earl of
Bothwell. Either foolishly (and dangerously)
written by her, or else a clever forgery
by Scottish Protestant lords, designed to
incriminate – no-one knows.*

CHAPTER THREE

ROYALTY, ROMANCE AND RELIGION

Young, tall, slim, beautiful, charismatic, a fashion icon, unhappily married, longing for love, and tragically dead before her time. Heard all that somewhere before? No, we're not describing the late lamented Diana, Princess of Wales, but her distant ancestor, Mary Queen of Scots. Apart from their colouring (Diana was blonde, Mary had stunning red hair and golden eyes) the two royal ladies were unhappily similar in a surprising number of ways.

Edinburgh had been a royal capital city for over a century when Mary was born (at

Linlithgow, about 20 miles (32 km) away, in 1542). And, for most of her time in Scotland, Mary's home was Edinburgh's Holyrood Palace. As we saw in Chapter 2, Holyrood was first built between 1501 and 1528, to replace the old royal guest-room at the abbey, by Mary's grandfather James IV, then beautified by her energetic father, James V. Compared with rough, rugged Edinburgh Castle, Holyrood had comfortable royal apartments, grand reception halls and ornamental gardens. (Mary later added an archery practice range, and not one but two organs.) King James's Holyrood also boasted a menagerie – with real lions and a smelly civet – a library, resident musicians, poets and historians, an engineering workshop (James V was fascinated by ballistics, and made his own fireworks), a mint for striking coins, well-stocked hunting grounds, a blacksmith's forge and a special horse-powered machine for polishing royal suits of armour.

Holyrood was fashionable; it was built in the latest, international, Renaissance style. With his nose perhaps a little out of joint, chronicler Robert Lindsay recorded that James V:

'...plenished the country with all kind of craftsmen out of other countries, as Frenchmen, Spaniards, Dutch men, and Englishmen, which were all cunning craftsmen, every man for his own hand. Some were gunners, wrights, carvers, painters, masons, smiths, harnessmakers [armourers], tapesters [tapestry makers], broudsters [embroiderers], taylors, cunning chirurgeons, apothecaries, with all other kind of craftsmen to apparel his palaces...'

In Edinburgh, these foreign experts were hard at work between 1528 and 1536. Alas, just eight years later, much of their work was destroyed when an English army landed at Leith and advanced into the city. The Provost offered a ransom, but the English commanders refused. They were under strict orders to:

'Put all to fire and sword, burn Edinburgh, so razed and defaced when you have sacked and gotten what ye can of it, as there may remain forever a perpetual memory of the vengeance of God lightened upon [the Scots] for their falsehood and disloyalty.'

Why were the English so aggressive and vindictive? Because of Mary – although, at only two years of age, she can hardly be said to have been personally at fault. She had become Queen of Scotland at six days old, when James V died of a broken heart after hearing of the Scots' defeat (by the English) at the battle of Solway Moss – or, less romantically, from drinking polluted water. James had at least nine illegitimate children, but Mary was his only surviving lawful heir. Ambitious King Henry VIII of England, together with leading Protestant Scots, proposed a marriage between Mary and his son, Prince Edward. This would give England control over Scotland; the English would also be able to choose Scotland's religion.

Not surprisingly, Mary's mother, French Catholic noblewoman Marie of Guise, was unhappy with this plan. So were her supporters among powerful Scottish Catholic families, and her royal allies overseas. They repudiated any marriage arranged for Mary. In return, from 1543 to 1550, Henry VIII launched cross-border raids to make the Scots change their minds: the so-called 'Rough Wooing'.

The English attacked Edinburgh again in 1547, but Marie of Guise was not a woman to be bullied. The next year, six-year-old Mary was shipped off to France, and betrothed to the French Dauphin (Crown Prince).

It was a strange match – the Dauphin was dim and sickly, Mary was lively and attractive. But she was said to be heartbroken when her young husband died. No longer politically useful to the French royal family, and still mourning her mother (Marie of Guise died in 1560), Mary returned to Edinburgh in 1561 to reclaim her Scottish throne.

From the start, things did not go well. Arriving at the crack of dawn, at shell-shocked Leith, in thick fog, Mary had to shelter in a townsman's house, because her apartments at Holyrood were not ready. The Edinburgh streets were as smelly and noisy as ever – a shock to Mary's delicate senses, which had grown accustomed to the refined, elegant perfumes and sweet music of the French royal court.

Disgraceful!

May nane pass throw your principall
   gaittis
For stink of haddockis and of scattis,
For cryis of carlinges and debattis
For fensum flytingis of defamis
Think ye not schame
Before strangeris of all estatis
That sic dishonour hurt your name?

Scotland's Makar (national poet)
William Dunbar, To the Merchantis of
Edinburgh, c. 1500.

No-one will walk along your main streets
Because they stink of haddock and skate [a fish that smells strongly of
ammonia]
Or because of the shouts of quarrelsome old women
Or rough insults and abuse hurled by rogues.
Don't you think it's shameful,
In front of all kinds of strangers,
That such dishonour damages your good name?

Even so, the Edinburgh crowds greeted Mary warmly, in spite of the fact that they favoured the new Protestant brand of the Christian faith. The city's religious leaders were not so tolerant, however. There were angry meetings, held at Holyrood, between staunchly Catholic Mary and stern Protestant preacher John Knox (1514–1572). Knox asserted that he must speak God's word and warn Mary against her sin and error. Mary, shocked and scared by such 'democratic' criticism, refused to give up her Catholic faith – and was, at the end, reduced to tears of sheer fury and frustration. She feared this was an argument she could not win; Edinburgh was on Knox's side.

John Knox speaks his mind to Mary Queen of Scots, 1564

The religious story so far

Like the rest of Europe, Scotland had seen its fair share of religious quarrels between traditionalist Catholics and reforming Protestants in the years before Mary was born. In 1543, Protestants were burned alive at St Andrews and in Edinburgh; in retaliation, Catholic Cardinal Beaton was murdered in 1546 at Scotland's ancient religious centre, St Andrews – and his mutilated body was hung out of his palace's upper window.

Elsewhere, poets satirised the 'abominations' and 'harlotries' of church leaders, monks and nuns. Wandering preachers called on Scots people to turn away from authoritarian Rome and follow the new, reformed religion, in which every man or woman would be equal in the eyes of God. Bibles in English were smuggled from England into Edinburgh; so were scholarly religious works from Geneva, the home of the stern doctrine of Predestination, which saw some souls as saved from hell by divine will, while others were eternally damned.

In 1557, gangs of hot-headed Protestants seized the statue of St Giles as it was being carried through the streets on its annual saint's day procession. They threw it into the Nor' Loch, then hauled it out and tried to burn it. Around the same time, a 'godly band' (group of campaigners), the Lords of the Congregation, was formed, to call for freedom to worship in the Protestant way.

In 1558 there were riots when Catholic Marie of Guise summoned the Lords of the Congregation to appear before her. Angry mobs attacked monasteries and churches, smashing statues, shrines, and at least one royal tomb. In 1559, Marie fled from Edinburgh, and the Lords of the Congregation took control of Holyrood.

English king Henry VIII strengthened Protestant power; Marie relied on France for support, sending secret messages, once she was safely back in Edinburgh Castle, written in invisible ink. In 1560, thousands of French troops built a state-of-the-art fortress at Leith. Sent by Henry, Protestant English gunners arrived and began to smash the fort and port with cannon. But they were overpowered by the Scots and French and retreated to Edinburgh. There, they were slaughtered by the citizens – who shared their religion but had not forgiven earlier English invasions. Marie of Guise, looking out from the castle at dead bodies in the streets, is said (by her Protestant enemies) to have rejoiced at 'such a fair tapestry...'

Meanwhile, elsewhere in Edinburgh, the Lords of the Congregation had persuaded the Scottish Parliament to support the Protestant cause. Marie of Guise died in June 1560; within a couple of months, advised by John Knox, an assembly of fourteen earls, six bishops, nineteen lords, twenty one abbots, twenty-two burgh representatives and over a hundred powerful landowners had approved a Confession of Faith, setting up a new system of Protestant doctrine and worship in Scotland. Six months after that, as we saw on page 79, Mary Queen of Scots arrived from France.

However, as Knox had warned, Mary's choice of friends – and husbands – soon had Edinburgh up in arms. In 1565, she married weak, handsome, vain, mean, arrogant, high-born, vicious, violent Henry, Lord Darnley, in Holyrood Chapel. Whilst not exactly love at first sight, 'Her Majesty took well with him, and said that he was the lustiest and best proportioned long [tall] man that she had seen.' Darnley did his duty, soon getting Mary with child, but was angered by her refusal to grant him the crown matrimonial, which would have made him king if she died. He also showed support for Mary's political enemies, the Protestant party. They, of course, were using him for their own ends – to attack her.

Less than a year after the wedding, Darnley became jealous of Mary's Italian secretary, David Rizzio. Late one night, he led a party of Protestant nobles to Holyrood, to surprise a very pregnant Mary, Rizzio and their servants as they sat in Mary's private apartment. Terrified, Rizzio clung to Mary's skirts, but the assassins held a dagger to her throat, threatening to kill her and her unborn child if she called for help. Then they dragged

Rizzio away, and stabbed him 56 times. Mary and Darnley were held prisoners in their own palace. To save their skins, they agreed to work together for a while. They escaped, rallied Mary's supporters, and returned to issue orders that anyone accusing Darnley of Rizzio's murder would be executed. For extra safety, Mary moved to Edinburgh Castle in June 1566 to give birth – to a fine son. Darnley refused to attend the christening, and, still angry at being denied a kingly crown, helped spread false rumours that he was not the child's father.

A gory reminder

Until the 19th century, Holyrood Palace servants painted the steps of one chamber with raddle (red ochre, used to mark sheep), claiming that this was Rizzio's blood, that could never be washed away. Visitors could inspect the stain, for a fee...

On pain of death

Done something dreadful? Got on the wrong side of the king, the burgh council or the leaders of the church? Then it's likely that, in past centuries, you'd end up at Edinburgh's Mercat Cross in the High Street, being put to death in an extremely horrible way. Crowds of townsfolk would come to watch you die; for them, it was a welcome holiday. Here are just a few examples:

- **1437 Walter, Earl of Atholl**. Killed the king (James I)! Execution lasted for three days:

  Day 1 – Hauled up high on a crane, then dropped to the ground. Many bones broken.

  Day 2 – Crowned with a red-hot iron 'crown', then dragged through the streets of Edinburgh.

  Day 3 – 'Drawn' (cut open, heart and intestines pulled out and burned). Finally beheaded. His head was fixed to a long pole and carried through the burgh. Bits of his body were sent to other towns in Scotland.

  Atholl's fellow-conspirator (his grandson) was repeatedly stabbed with red-hot iron spikes, and then beheaded.

- **1541 James Hamilton**. Accused of breaking into King James V's bedchamber. He was beheaded (fairly quick and painless – the privilege of noble rank) then and 'quartered' (butchered into four or more pieces). His body parts were hung on gates and walls around the city and left to rot – the usual fate of traitors.

- **1564 The Maiden.** No, not a young victim, but a new, humane, killing machine. An early form of guillotine, the Maiden had a sharp blade weighted with a lump of lead to make it fall quickly. According to legend, plans to introduce the Maiden to Edinburgh were first made by James Douglas, Earl of Morton, who ran the Scottish government while King James VI was a child. Certainly, in a cruel twist of fate, Morton was executed by the Maiden in 1581.

- **1588 John Dickson.** Accused of murdering his father. More new technology was used for his execution, but this time, crueller than ever. Dickson was stretched out on a wooden frame, then beaten all over with an iron bar. As many bones as possible were broken, then he was left lingering all night, to die.

- **1591 Dr John Fian.** Schoolmaster, said to be 'a sorcerer'. Tortured for days, in the bad old ways, to try to make him confess. A rope was bound round his head and pulled tighter, tighter. His legs were crushed in a wood and iron cage (nicknamed the 'boot'). His fingernails were pulled out, and needles were pushed full-length into his flesh. Reportedly terrified by a vision of the Devil, Fian refused to say sorry for his 'sins'. He was burnt alive, without the mercy of being strangled first, like most other witches.

Why did Edinburgh's leaders kill and torture criminals? Why did so many people come to watch? Were they all monsters? No, not really. Past powerful people lived in fear of a challenge to their authority, from noble rivals, foreign enemies, cunning conspirators or an out-of-control burgh mob. They believed that murder, riot, rebellion and other serious crimes were against God's laws. The horrible punishments were designed to 'pay back' wrong-doers for their crimes, and as an awful warning to deter others.

And the cheering crowds? Partly, they, too, believed that law-and-order was good for their community. Partly, they were curious. Partly, they enjoyed watching bear-baiting and dog-fighting, and a well-staged execution was rather similar. And a death-day always meant time off work, and a chance to relax with friends and family.

Edinburgh High Street in the 19th century.
The Mercat Cross – of bloody memory – was
rebuilt close by, in 1885.

Worse scandal was to follow. In the dead of night, in February 1567, a house at Kirk o' Field, on the outskirts of Edinburgh, was demolished by a sudden violent explosion. Darnley's lifeless body was found in the garden. Mary had been to visit him earlier that evening, but left before midnight. Did she know of the plot to blow up her husband? Many people thought so. Darnley's father arranged for the chief suspect, James Hepburn, Earl of Bothwell, to be put on trial in Edinburgh. But Bothwell's men, armed to the teeth, thronged the streets outside the court and he was acquitted.

When, soon afterwards, Mary rushed to visit Bothwell, even her friends were appalled. Just a few weeks later, Bothwell kidnapped Mary. Probably, the attack was agreed in advance – although presumably not the rape that followed. Pregnant again, Mary married Bothwell in a Protestant ceremony in Holyrood's Great Hall. This was the final straw, for Edinburgh and for much of Scotland. Mary was 'an hoor', perhaps a murderess, and had betrayed her own religion. No-one wanted Bothwell as their king. Edinburgh streets sported cartoons of Mary as a naked mermaid – sailors' code for a prostitute. Scots Protestant lords raised an army; Mary's followers were defeated at Carberry Hill near Edinburgh on 15 June 1567.

Mary was arrested and left Edinburgh as a prisoner, never to return. She was forced to abdicate, fled to England, and her baby son, James VI, became king. Bothwell escaped to Denmark, where he too was put in prison, went mad, and died, in chains.

Back home in Scotland, there was more fighting: 'an intestine war in the bowels of commonwealth'. On one side were Mary's (mostly Catholic) supporters, backed by European royal families, claiming that she was still Scotland's lawful ruler and hoping for her return. On the other side were Protestant supporters of young King James VI, led by Mary's illegitimate half-brother, James Stewart, Earl of Moray.

The city of Edinburgh was caught in the crossfire. In 1571, the King's troops bombarded Holyrood with cannon, while the Captain of the Castle promised loyalty to Moray and began building work – the Half Moon Battery – to strengthen the castle's defences. But Moray was murdered in 1570, by Mary's supporters, laid in state at Holyrood, and buried at St Giles. Thinking the King was losing the battle, the Captain of the Castle changed sides, arresting the Provost of Edinburgh and compelling the townsfolk to obey.

The King's troops hurried to Leith, and in April 1571, the 'Lang Siege' began. It lasted for two years. Cannonballs from both sides crashed into city houses; over 100 townsfolk were killed. The castle defenders ran short of food; the King's troops poisoned the well providing water for the castle. Then England's Queen Elizabeth sent some massive cannon. After days of continuous bombardment, the castle defenses collapsed. The Castle Captain was horribly executed. At long last there was peace.

The King's procession

Picture the scene. It's 1579, eight years since the Lang Siege, and – politically speaking – Edinburgh has quietened down. Young King James VI is now a teenager (he's 13), and it's time, and safe enough, for him to make a grand ceremonial entry into his capital, and take up residence at Holyrood (where he eventually accumulates a staff of 600!). The burgh leaders are determined to impress the king and his powerful advisors. They collect £4,000 in tax from the townspeople, who spend weeks rehearsing actors and dancers, stitching costumes, building stage sets and devising props (a winged god, descending from the clouds! a revolving wheel of fortune, powered by fireworks!). Their aim? A lavish display – with a not-so-subtle message. This is their chance to tell James how they expect him to rule:

• The King's procession enters the city through the West Port (gate). James is greeted by viols, trumpets, singers, and a short play on the theme of wisdom and justice: the Bible story of the Judgement of Solomon.

• Next (to keep things friendly), Cupid, god of love, flies down from the clouds and presents James with the golden keys of the city.

• At the Tolbooth, James is greeted by four young ladies, dressed (probably) as Prudence, Justice, Temperance and Courage.

• At St Giles' Kirk, the figure of Dame Religion invites him inside, to hear a (Protestant) sermon.

• By now, James – and everyone else – could do with some refreshment. And the burgh leaders have to keep the townsfolk happy. So Bacchus, god of Good Cheer, steps out from behind the Mercat (Merchant) Cross – and Edinburgh's drinking fountains flow with wine.

• Heading east, past the Tron, James 'Meets the Ancestors'. He's confronted by portraits of past Scottish rulers, and his family tree. A reminder that he should try to rule like the best of them – if not, he might share the grisly fate of some others.

• As the procession leaves the walled burgh, and heads down Canongate towards Holyrood, a display of planets decorates the Netherbow (gate). A semi-mythical figure, King Ptolemy, explains. See! The heavens have smiled on our king (and let's hope they'll continue to guide him wisely).

• Nearly home now. But just one more message to make sure that James stays on the Protestant straight and narrow. At Canongate Cross, he's greeted by a 'brief fable', showing the overthrow of the Pope and the ending of Roman Catholic worship.

A walk on the wild side

James's triumphal entry to Edinburgh was obviously quite a day. But what was life like for the ordinary men, women and children of the burgh for the rest of the time? How did they survive invasions, royal romances, riots, rebellions, religious reformations – and much more?

At least one 16th-century visitor, poet William Dunbar, painted a very grim picture. He sees Edinburgh as socially divided, full of beggars but controlled by rich merchants, who are uncharitable, selfish, greedy, ungodly. The whole town sets a bad example to the rest of the nation!

To the Merchantis of Edinburgh

Your Burgh of beggaris is ane nest ;
To schout thai swenyouris [scroungers] will nocht
   rest;
All honest folk they do molest,
Sa piteouslie thai cry and rame.

Think ye nocht schame
That for the poore has nothing drest [ready to
   offer],
In hurt and slander of your name ?

Your profifeit dailie dois incress,
Your godlie workis less and less ;
Through streittis [streets] nane may mak progress
For cry of cruikit, blind, and lame.

Think ye nocht schame
That ye sic substance [so much wealth] dois possess.
And will nocht win ane bettir name?

Sen, for the Court and the Session,
The great repair of this regioun
Is in your Burgh, thairfoir be boun
To mend all faults that ar to blame.

And eschew schame :
Gif thai pas to ane uther toun,
Ye will decay, and your great name !

William Dunbar (lived around 1500)

Dunbar is harsh, but 16th- and 17th-century Edinburgh could be a pretty tough place to live. After James VI inherited the crown of England from his distant cousin Queen Elizabeth I in 1603, he moved south to London. Although promising to return, he only did so once, for a meeting of the Scottish Parliament in 1617. For a while, Edinburgh was left reeling. James's courtiers and servants at Holyrood had been very good customers. Many businesses went bankrupt; at night, mobs of the unemployed, beggars and vagabonds gathered 'to pass their time in all kinds of riot and filthy lechery'.

Even long before this, Edinburgh streets could be very violent. The fighting flared up suddenly:

In 1567 '. . . the Laird of Airth and the Laird of Weems met on the High Gate (street) of Edinburgh, and they and their followers fought a very bloody skirmish, where there were many hurt on both sides with shot of pistol.'

This sounds very similar to the street battle in 1520 that became known as 'Cleanse the Causey' (causeway). Two powerful politicians, Douglas and Hamilton (a former Provost of Edinburgh) were feuding. Each brought 500 armed supporters with them into the burgh. The result? A massacre – maybe 300 men were killed, and, until they were 'cleansed', Edinburgh's narrow wynds ran with blood.

Schoolboy shoots magistrate!

In 1595, the pupils of Edinburgh's ancient Royal High School staged a lock-in, in protest at being punished for bad behaviour in the class of their new teacher, Hercules Rollock.

Edinburgh magistrate, rich merchant Baillie MacMorran, was called in. But he was fatally shot in the head by one of the pupils, William Sinclair. Together with six other boys, Sinclair was sent to prison. But he was soon set free; his grandfather was one of Scotland's most powerful nobles.

That's enough of gangs and gun-culture. The third problem Edinburgh shared with some troubled modern cities was overcrowding. The high walls enclosing the town – work on a new wall, known as the Flodden Wall, started in 1513 – meant that there was very little room for new buildings. Where possible, 'lands' (apartment blocks) were expanded by rebuilding upwards. Edinburgh is said to have had the world's first skyscrapers – the tallest land was 14 storeys high. They collapsed, quite often.

Inside each land, apartments were not the same. Shopkeepers occupied the ground floor; rich merchants and professional or landed families lived in well-furnished sets of rooms on the first, second or third floors, while the upper storeys and attics, which were draughty, smoky and a long climb from the street, housed large numbers of poor, ordinary people. Servants sometimes slept in passageways or even on the stairs; shivering beggars slept rough, out of doors, in Edinburgh's biting winds. Only the very grandest noble families had their own private houses. Everyone else lived close to their neighbours – a fine gentlemen leaving his land might have to dodge customers from the rowdy ground-floor tavern, or step over a beggar sleeping in his doorway.

As our gentleman walked along, he would almost certainly meet several people he knew well. Although Edinburgh's population grew – from around 8,000 in 1600 to 35,000 in 1700 – it was always an intimate community. He would also, alas, encounter Edinburgh's lamentable lack of sanitation. There were no drains or sewers under the streets, no litterbins or refuse collections, and no bathrooms. Many people just dumped their refuse anywhere they could, and used gutters or dark corners as toilets. So, of course, did Edinburgh's horses, donkeys, dogs, cats, rats and mice. Some families even kept a pig, tied close to their front door, to scavenge and grow fat among the stinking rubbish.

Morning and evening, servants would tip brimming lavatory buckets out of high windows, with a cheerful cry of 'gardyloo' (French *gardez l'eau*, 'look out for the water!'). The resulting puddles in the streets, and splashes on clothes, were nicknamed 'Edinburgh flowers'. Even the most admiring visitors found the smell of the streets quite unbearable: 'No smells were ever equal to Scotch smells.' Others said that to live in such a filthy place, Edinburgh folk must be a 'most nasty, sluttish and slothful people'.

There was no piped water in Edinburgh until the late 17th century (see page 60), and, when it rained, dirt was washed down steep narrow streets into the Nor' Loch – a valley at the northern foot of Castle Rock that had been artificially deepened (or maybe dammed) to create a stagnant, shallow defensive moat. By the 16th century, Nor' Loch was a sinister place of dark deeds – and a breeding ground for many diseases. Unwanted babies were sometimes disposed of there, men and women accused of sexual crimes, nagging wives and cheating traders were all tied to the burgh ducking stool and dipped in the Loch's filthy waters. Occasionally, women accused of witchcraft were bound and thrown in, too. If they sank they were innocent, but dead. If they floated, they were guilty – and executed.

With so much dirt all around, it is no surprise that Edinburgh suffered from deadly epidemics of smallpox, dysentery, typhoid and flu. From the 14th to the 17th centuries, there were also outbreaks of plague. The worst was in 1645, when terrified families locked themselves inside their homes and burgh life came to a standstill.

From 1529 onwards, burgh leaders tried to control the spread of plague by driving victims and their contacts out to makeshift hovels on the Burgh Muir (an open space south of the walls). Anyone trying to escape this quarantine was hanged. Infected houses were washed and fumigated by highly paid cleaners; in 1645 special plague doctors were hired. At long last, in 1686, the Scottish Parliament passed a law to make Edinburgh street-cleaning compulsory.

Moral pollution?

As well as fearing physical diseases, from the mid 16th century, burgh leaders were also afraid of spiritual corruption. The Reformed Kirk appointed seizers – religious police – at first to enforce attendance at kirk services on Sundays, and later zealously to investigate what they believed to be all kinds of moral crimes. Preachers thundered against idleness, drunkenness, unlawful sex, political protest, and disobedient wives and servants.

By around 1650, because anyone who could afford it employed a serving girl or two, there were 10 women in Edinburgh to every 7 men. Perhaps as a consequence, there were also a large number of out-of-wedlock pregnancies. Getting pregnant was a moral crime; so was concealing a pregnancy or birth. Offenders were made to sit on the shameful 'stool of repentance' in front of the whole kirk, every Sunday for weeks or months. Almost certainly, they lost their jobs, as well, and became beggars (or worse). If they killed their newly-born child – as many felt they had to do – they were executed.

Even upper-class women did not escape punishment. In a famous and tragic case, Jean Livingston, Lady Warriston, was executed for arranging the murder of her husband. Wed at 15, to an older man whom she hated, Lady Warriston was very beautiful. Her husband was jealous and violent, frequently beating and injuring her and accusing her of infidelity. By July 1600, Lady Warriston could stand it no longer; she sent a manservant, aided and abetted by her old nurse, to kill her husband. The servant escaped, but lady Warriston and her nurse were arrested and imprisoned:

'...scho [she] wes tare [taken] to the Girth Crosse upon the 5 day of Julii, and her heid struk fra her bodie at the Cannagait... quha diet [she died] verie patiently. Her nurische [nurse] wes brunt [burned] at the same tyme, at 4 houres in the morneing...'

The Ballad of Lady Warriston

Down by yon garden green
Sae merrily as she gaes;
She has twa [two] weel-made feet,
And she trips upon her taes.

She has twa weel-made feet,
Far better is her hand;
She's as jimp [slender] in the middle
As ony willow-wand.

'Gif [If] ye will do my bidding,
At my bidding for to be,
It's I [Lord Warriston] will make you lady
Of a' the lands you see.'

He [Warriston] spak a word in jest;
Her answer wasna good;
He threw a plate at her face,
Made it a' gush out o blood.

She wasna frae [had not gone out of] her chamber
A step but barely three,
When up and at her richt hand
There stood Man's Enemy [the Devil].

'Gif ye will do my bidding,
At my bidding for to be,
I'll learn you a wile
Avenged for to be.'

The Foul Thief [Devil] knotted the tether,
She [Lady Warriston] lifted his head on hie,
The nourice [nursemaid] drew the knot
That gard [made] lord Waristoun die.

Then word is gane to Leith,
Also to Edinburgh town,
That the lady had killd the laird,
The laird o Waristoun.

'Tak aff, tak aff my hood,
But lat my petticoat be;
Put my mantle oer my head,
For the fire [of Hell] I downa [dare not] see.

'Now, a' ye gentle maids,
Tak warning now by me,
And never marry ane [anyone]
But wha [Unless he] pleases your ee [eye].

'For he married me for love,
But I married him for fee [rank and money];
And sae brak out [this caused] the feud
That gard my dearie die.'

Robert Jamieson, Popular Ballads and
Songs from Tradition, *1806*

The unusually early hour of Lady Warriston's execution was a special privilege, to give her privacy and avoid scandal for her high-ranking family. But normally, Edinburgh executions – of which there were a great many – were popular public entertainments. Especially if the victims had been accused of … WITCHCRAFT!

Don't panic?

From the 15th to the 17th centuries, all Europe shared a moral panic about witches. Why? There have been religious, pyschiatric and sociological explanations. Whatever the reason, the panic was real and very nasty, and Scotland suffered worse than most. Even King James VI feared witchcraft and its dangers to his kingdom. His book, *Daemonologie* (1597), helped to fuel the hunt for witches.

Only a few sensible Scottish souls, such as Reginal Scot, author of *The Discoveries of Witchcraft* (1584), argued that there might be a rational explanation for storms, sicknesses, and other misfortunes said to have been called up by witches. Such arguments were largely ignored. Everyone – even accused women in fear of their lives – believed in the supernatural. And in traditional healing rituals, and strange herbal cures.

In Edinburgh, around 300 people were executed for witchcraft. A few were men, including Dr James Reid (died 1603). The doctor was accused of learning his medical skills from the devil, and of consorting with Old Nick on Arthur's Seat. However, most alleged witches were women. King James said that this was because they were naturally frailer than men.

The most celebrated witch coven was alleged to have sailed in sieves (how else?) from Leith to North Berwick (both near Edinburgh), and there conducted grisly rituals – dancing in churchyards, collecting venom from toads, tying bits of dead bodies to cats and then throwing the mewing bundles into the sea – to try to wreck the King's ship as it sailed home from Denmark.

Typically, witches were strangled (so their souls could escape from their bodies, and have a last chance to flee the devil) and then burned. Today, a water-feature known as the Witches' Fountain marks the spot close to Edinburgh Castle where all these unfortunates were executed.

An accusation of witchcraft was also a very handy tool to use against enemies. It was almost impossible to disprove. For example, as part of the centuries-old feud between the royal Stewarts and the ambitious Douglas family, Jane Douglas, Lady Glamis, was burned as a witch in Edinburgh in 1537, on the false testimony of King James V.

North Berwick witches, 1591

The Killing Times

Later, in the mid-17th century, Edinburgh saw a fresh orgy of bloodshed – from yet another deadly mixture of religious and political motives.

Remember the Lords of the Congregation? (see page 82) In 1560, they had persuaded a (fairly willing) Scottish Parliament to make the Protestant Kirk the national church of Scotland. But in 1618, James VI had bullied the Kirk into accepting bishops (high-ranking church leaders) – though for political, rather than religious reasons: the bishops would obey James.

However, when James VI's son became Charles I in 1625, old religious quarrels heated up, and quickly.

How to to win (scottish) friends and influence people (not)

- Charles wanted bishops, too, and Church of England prayers and rituals.
- Charles imposed crippling taxes on Scotland – when Edinburgh traders were going through a bad time.
- Charles threatened to take away Scottish noble families' land.
- Charles ignored the Scottish Parliament in Edinburgh. Instead, he ruled Scotland from London through a team of hand-picked grandees.

In 1637, there were riots in Edinburgh when St Giles Kirk ministers reluctantly began to use King Charles's English-style prayer-book. Old Edinburgh market wifie Jenny Geddes threw her folding stool at the minister's head: 'De'il colic the wame o' ye, fause thief; daur ye say Mass in my lug?'

[God rot your guts, you cheating thief; how dare you say Mass in my ear!]

The bishop was pelted with Bibles, sticks and stones; angry crowds stormed through Edinburgh's streets for hours afterwards.

Signed in blood

The next year, a group of Scottish Protestant nobles and Edinburgh-based lawyers decided that it was time for a new Covenant. It was to go nationwide, a huge petition to King Charles asking for an end to English-style 'errors' of worship, and for the Kirk to become entirely Presbyterian. (Ministers were to be chosen by local congregations, not by kings.) The Covenanters also asked for free, effective Scottish Parliaments to be called, to govern their own nation.

Many Scots who signed the Covenant used their own blood. It was a bad omen, for soon Scotland – and Edinburgh – were at war. The Covenanters' armies joined the Parliamentary side in the English Civil War. After years of bitter battles – during which the Covenanters captured Charles I and handed him over to the English – the English Parliamentarians cut off the King's head in 1649.

Much as they disliked King Charles, the Scots were horrified. The Scottish Parliament quickly proclaimed his son, Charles II, as king

– but, not trusting their new young monarch, they also executed the Scottish royalist leader, who had fought against the Covenanters. His name? James Graham, Marquess of Montrose – and he was killed very horribly. Anticipating this, in his Edinburgh prison cell, he wrote the following lines:

Let them bestow on every airth [direction] a limb,
Then open all my veings, that I may swim
To thee, my Maker, in that crimson lake;
Then place my parboiled head upon a stake,
Scatter my ashes, strew them in the air.
Lord, since Thou knowest where all these atoms
 are,
I'm hopefull Thou'lt recover all my dust,
And confident Thou'lt raise me with the just.

Worse, if possible, was to follow. Scotland's coronation of Charles II angered the English Parliament's army. Led by Oliver Cromwell, no less, the English invaded Scotland. Members of the Scottish Parliament, the Burgh Council of Edinburgh and the Session (leaders) of the Kirk all ran away. Cromwell captured Edinburgh without a fight; even the castle garrison surrendered.

Elsewhere, outside Edinburgh, Scotland suffered badly in the fighting that followed between Cromwell and Scottish royalists. But Cromwell died, and in 1660 the English and Scottish Parliaments both called on Charles II to return from exile. Covenanters were now on the losing side: Charles II declared that Covenanting was illegal. In Edinburgh, people were hanged just for listening to a Covananter sermon.

From 1666 to 1679, there was war between the Covenanters and King Charles. After a crushing defeat at Bothwell Bridge, near Glasgow, 1,200 bruised and battered survivors of the Covenanter army were marched to Edinburgh, and locked up in Greyfriars Churchyard. This peaceful place now became one of the world's first concentration camps. The Covenanters were fed just 100 grams of bread a day; they had no warm clothing or shelter, although it was winter. They died of cold and hunger, or after being cruelly tortured – the 'boot', that slowly crushed their legs was a favourite instrument. Their leaders were executed. About 250 'fortunate' survivors were shipped to the Americas, to be slaves. But their ship sank on the journey, and many drowned.

Before his time

An era when religious anxiety, mixed with intolerance, was the ruling sentiment of Edinburgh was perhaps not the best time to declare that you were a non-believer. Yet that is what a hot-headed Edinburgh University student named Thomas Aitkenhead did in 1697. He boldly – stupidly – made clear his contempt for religious authority:

'It is a principle innate [inborn]...to every man to have an insatiable inclination to the truth, and to seek for it as for hid treasure.'

Aitkenhead was signing his own death warrant. The law-courts gave the Edinburgh Kirk the chance to reprieve him, but they refused. He was hanged, for blasphemy, aged just 20. Most Scots were shocked.

However grim the living conditions and savage the political struggles, life in Edinburgh could also be very enjoyable. Here is a complaint made in 1719 by killjoy Edinburgh Kirk leaders about the way in which Edinburgh folk liked to spend their Sundays:

'A great number take an unaccountable liberty . . . by standing in companies in the streets, misspending their time in idle discourse, vain and useless communications . . . withdrawing from the city . . . to take their recreations in walking through the fields, parks, links [seaside grassland], meadows . . . And by entering taverns, ale-houses, milk-houses, gardens or other places, to drink, tipple, or otherwise misspend any part thereof; by giving and receiving civil [polite, friendly] visits . . . and by idly gazing out of windows . . . Yea, some have arrived at the height of impiety, as not to be ashamed of washing in waters, and swimming in rivers upon the holy Sabbath.'

> *quoted in James Buchan,*
> Capital of the Mind 2003

To later generations, it all sounds quite fun – and quite innocent – but the Edinburgh churchmen feared that such amusements, together, of course, with the 'promiscuous dancing of men with women' would bring down 'the wrath of God on them and their land'.

'I like this place exceedingly. It unites good libraries, liberally managed; learned men without any system [purpose] than that of pursuing truth; very good general society; [and – tut, tut, Reverend Sir!] large healthy virgins, with mild pleasing countenances, and white swelling breasts...'

English visitor to Edinburgh, the Reverend Sydney Smith, 1798

CHAPTER four

THE 'ATHENS OF THE NORTH'

O n 3 October 1706, Edinburgh was not a happy place to be. Surly crowds surged and grumbled in the streets. Soldiers stood tense and wary, waiting for trouble; there had already been riots. All Edinburgh was watching – for the last time ever, so far as anyone could tell – the 'Riding of Parliament': the grand procession of the King (or more usually, his deputy, the High Commissioner), nobles, clergy and burgh representatives, riding on horseback from the Palace of Holyrood to Parliament Hall. That splendid building, completed in 1632, stood at the very heart of Edinburgh, close to the Castle and the Kirk of St Giles. It was the centre of Scotland's political life, a proud symbol of Scots independence, and an imposing ornament to Edinburgh, the Scottish capital.

But not for much longer. On 1 May 1707, *An Act Ratifying and Approving the Treaty of Union of the Two Kingdoms of SCOTLAND and ENGLAND* passed into law. It was, as the royal High Commissioner remarked, the 'end of an auld sang'. And it was celebrated (if that is the word) by Edinburgh church bells playing another old Scottish tune: 'Why should I be sad on my wedding day?'

From 1707, there would be no separate Scottish Parliament; MPs elected in Scotland would have to travel to Westminster (the journey by coach took a over a week) to try to make their voices heard there. All important decisions, from taxation to war, would be made by the UK government in London. Scotland would have no veto. Any Scotsman hoping for a serious career in politics or administration would have to travel to London, too.

And, although the Act of Union allowed the Scottish people to keep their national Protestant church and ancient legal system, Scotland was in real danger of becoming a backwater, far away from the centre of British economic and political power. And, now that Edinburgh was no longer a 'proper' capital city, would it be ignored, forgotten, irrelevant?

Union with England made some Scottish politicians rich – as poet Robert Burns scornfully said, they were 'bought and sold for English gold'. But it angered many ordinary Scots people. In particular, the merchants of Edinburgh feared that union with England would ruin their trade: ships and sailors from northern Engand would take over.

The Queensberry Curse

James Douglas, second Duke of Queensberry (died 1711), belonged to one of the grandest old Scottish families. He served as High Commissioner in 1702, 1703 and 1706, and played an important part in persuading members of the Scottish Parliament to agree to union with England. In return, he received vast sums of English government money and English noble titles as a reward. Not surprisingly, he became very unpopular with many people in Scotland, especially the Edinburgh poor.

In January 1707, hostile feelings were running so high that Queensberry only dared venture out with a bodyguard of servants. Just one lad stayed behind at Queensberry House in Canongate, to keep the fires burning. When the Duke returned home, he found the boy – roasted over the kitchen fire, and half-eaten. The murderer? The Duke's nine-year-old son, James, Lord Drumlanrig.

Poor James had many physical problems, as well as mental disabilities. The sinister secret of Queensberry House, he was kept locked in a darkened room, with only one trusted servant to care for him. Somehow, he had escaped – and turned cannibal.

Was this a terible punishment on the Duke of Queensberry for selling Scotland?

Union with England:
Win or Lose?

Scots win:

- permission to trade with – and help govern – England's growing overseas empire

- no more harassment by English of Scottish ships and traders

- (limited) help with massive Scots debts after failure of overseas trading 'adventure', the Darien Scheme

- bribes for powerful top Scots who support the Union

- English taxation and involvement in English wars

- career opportunities for Scots in London.

Scots lose:

- Scottish monarch

- Scottish parliament

- Scottish flag, coins, weights and measures

- Scotland's name; it is replaced, for a while, by 'North Britain'

- power to make independent decisions for Scotland's future

- people: many ambitious and enterprising Scots leave, to seek their fortunes in London or British empire lands. Many Scots men join the British army;

- money. The London government imposes many new taxes

- and, last but not least, the Scots language.

'The dialect of the country most imperfect...'

Thomas Sheridan, actor and English-language speech coach in Edinburgh

Scots was – and is – more than just English spoken with a Scottish accent. And it's not an English dialect, but a separate language, with a long hitory. It developed slowly in Lowland Scotland, from around AD 600, by combining Old English, spoken in Northumbria (see page 38), with words from French, Flemish, German, Norse and Celtic languages. It was spoken by kings and queens, as well as ordinary folk. Together they created a powerfully expressive heritage of Scots poetry, prose and song.

However, after Union with England, Scots speakers were seen as backward and uncouth. Some Scots complained about being forced to speak Standard English if they wanted to be taken seriously:

'We who live in Scotland are obliged to study English like a dead language which we can understand but cannot speak...we are continually afraid of committing gross blunders.'

Others, keen to sound advanced and up to date, flocked to elocution lessons, given by an Irish actor in Edinburgh from 1761.

'Mister Miserable' and the Bonnie Prince

After the carnage of the 17th century, few Edinburgh people had much enthusiasm for war. But elsewhere in Scotland, there were skirmishes between British government troops and Jacobite[1] rebels. In 1689, Jacobites captured Edinburgh Castle. They were besieged by British government troops, but ran out of water and had to surrender. The castle was almost completely destroyed. In 1715, Jacobite armies marched through the burgh, but, chased by advancing government troops, hurried away after just two days.

The first Jacobite pretender (would-be king) was Prince James Edward Stewart. A uninspiring leader, his men called him Mister Miserable. James Edward's son, nicknamed Bonnie Prince Charlie, was indeed handsome, gracious, charming and brave – but inexperienced and inept. In 1745, his army entered Edinburgh with hardly a shot being fired. The prince received a rapturous welcome from the ladies; however, with an eye to business, or simply peace and good order, most of the menfolk in Edinburgh wished he would go way.

1. *Supporters of the exiled Stewart Scottish royal dynasty, that had ruled Scotland for centuries, and England since 1603.*

Bonnie Prince Charlie is Proclaimed King

An early historian relates how the prince was proclaimed King Charles III at Edinburgh Market Cross:

'The windows of the adjoining houses were filled with ladies, who testified the intensity of their feeling by straining their voices to the utmost pitch, and with outstretched arms waving white handkerchiefs in honour of the handsome young adventurer. Few gentlemen were, however, to be seen in the streets or at the windows, and even among the common people, there were not a few who preserved a stubborn silence.

'The effect of the ceremony was greatly heightened by the appearance of Mrs Murray of Broughton, a lady of great beauty, who, to show her devoted attachment to the cause of the Stuarts, decorated with a profusion of white ribbons, sat on horseback near the cross with a drawn sword in her hand…'

source: http://www.electricscotland.com/ history/charles/

Commercial capital

And yet, to everyone's surprise, the Union with England turned out to be good for Scotland, or at least, for its economy. Within about 50 years, the value of Scotland's exports had more than doubled. And, as a leading trading centre, Edinburgh shared in the general prosperity. The Bank of Scotland was founded in Edinburgh in 1695; the Royal Bank in 1727; the British Linen Company (also later a bank) in 1746. Brewers, weavers, frame-knitters, rope-makers and many other early industries flourished.

The first 'modern' hospital opened in 1729; a school for deaf children in 1760. There were at least three top-class boys' schools. Novelist (and spy) Daniel Defoe, visiting in the early 1720s, described many 'magnificent' houses, 'stately, high, and very handsome', and 'nobly built' streets, together with a market at the West Bow 'generally full of wholesale Traders, and those very considerable Dealers in Iron, Pitch, Tar, Oyl, Hemp, Flax, Linseed, Painters' Colours, Dyers, Drugs and Woods, and such like heavy Goods . . . And . . . most of them have also Warehouses in Leith, where they lay up the heavier Goods, and bring them hither, or sell them by Patterns and Samples . . .'

Defoe also mentioned Edinburgh's Physicians' Hall and Physick Garden (where plants to make medicines were grown), and a Museum, or 'Chamber of Rarities. Some of the items on display were not to be matched in Europe'. As further signs of prosperity, culture – and leisure – 18th-century Edinburgh also had:

- its own newspaper (from 1718);
- monthly *Scots Magazine* (1739 and still going strong);
- an Assembly Room (for dances, opened 1710);
- four printing presses in the 1740s and 27 by the 1770s, together with many publishers;
- a theatre (1747);
- a Penny Post service (1773);
- eight legal distilleries (and an estimated 400 illegal ones) (1770);
- stagecoach services to Glasgow (1749) and London (1753);
- and a golf club, ('The Gentlemen Golfers of Edinburgh', founded in 1744 – although Mary Queen of Scots was reported to have enjoyed the game centuries earlier, at Musselburgh, near Edinburgh, in 1567.

Shameful secrets

However, the old bloodstained Edinburgh was not yet dead – or buried. However *douce* or *weel-respectit* the newly-prosperous burgh might seem, it could still shock and scandalise. Many townsfolk probably felt that Edinburgh had seen it all when Thomas Weir went on trial in 1670. A leading member of a strict Covenanter group, Weir had suddenly confessed to a life of unspeakable crimes: child abuse, incest and worse. Not to be outdone, Weir's sister Jean had claimed that she was a witch, and that Weir's favourite walking stick was an evil magic wand. Edinburgh folk said that Weir must be mad, not bad, but the doctors pronounced him sane. He was strangled and burned outside the burgh walls; Jean was hanged on the gallows in the Grassmarket.

Half-Hangit Maggie

But now, in 1724, there was more to startle. Young wife Maggie Dickson, hanged in Edinburgh for killing her newborn child, sat up and started speaking in the cart taking her 'lifeless' body to be buried. The next day, she was well enough to walk home. Was it a miracle? Or had she seduced the hangman or the rope-maker before her execution?

No matter how Maggie managed to survive, her situation was an administrative nightmare. She had been pronounced legally dead, so she could not be tried, or hanged, again, for any crime. Her marriage had legally ended, too. All Edinburgh law officials could do was prosecute the hangman for inefficiency.

For once, Maggie's story had a happy ending. Her 'widower' remarried her, they had many more children, then for 40 years she ran a popular alehouse.

Rough justice?

Next, in 1736, John Porteous, captain of the Edinburgh Guard, was dragged from the Tolbooth prison and brutally lynched by an angry mob of, some said, over 4,000 townspeople. Why was this man, in charge of Edinburgh public order, locked up in his own gaol? And why did the crowd kill him?

Porteus had been on duty when one Andrew Wilson was hanged. Wilson, a well-liked man, had been led astray by criminal friends; together they had robbed a government customs house. Wilson's friends escaped; he stayed behind and took the blame.

Edinburgh poet and bookseller Allan Ramsay (see page 138) describes what happened next:

'All was hush, Psalms sung, prayers put up for a long hour and upwards and the man hang'd with all decency & quietnes. After he was cut down and the guard drawing up to go off, some unlucky boys threw a stone or two at the hangman, which is very common, on which the brutal Porteous ... let drive [fired] first himself amongst the inocent mob and commanded his men to folow his example which quickly cleansed the street but left three men, a boy and a woman dead upon the spot, besides several others wounded, some of whom are dead since. After this first fire he took it in his head ... to order annother voly & kill'd a taylor in a window three storys high, a young gentleman & a son of Mr Matheson the minister's and several more were dangerously wounded...'

More Culloden Papers, ed. D. Warrand,
Inverness, 1927

Porteous was arrested, tried and sentenced to death. But the distant London government felt that his strong-arm tactics should be rewarded, not punished, and considered releasing Porteous from prison. The Edinburgh mob had other ideas…

More than meets the eye

Perhaps the most surprising revelations came in 1788, with the trial of Deacon Brodie. The deacon (craft-guild leader) came from a very respectable family. He was a skilled cabinetmaker and locksmith, and a member of Edinburgh's ruling Council. Outwardly, he seemed decent, but secretly, he was leading a double, no, a treble, life. He drank heavily (and expensively), gambled, and was paying for two mistresses and many unofficial children. To fund this lavish lifestyle, the Deacon turned to crime.

Brodie's work naturally took him into the houses of rich people. Once there, he carefully made copies of the keys to their locks. All went well – although the crime-rate for night-time robberies rose sharply – until Brodie decided he needed cash, and lots of it, and robbed a government excise (tax) office. He was caught, escaped to Holland, was caught again, brought home, and hanged.

You pays your money and you takes your choice

Our final 18th–century shocker is curious, in that it probably seems more offensive to modern readers than it might have done to long-dead Edinburgh men. It is a printed directory of prostitutes, *Ranger's Impartial List of the Ladies of Pleasure in Edinburgh*, published in 1775. Its contents? A list of the burgh's professional ladies, outlining their physical perfections (or otherwise) and evaluating their – ahem – special skills.

A 'hotbed of genius'

By the 1750s, Scottish universities were among the best and most forward-thinking in the world. Edinburgh poet and librarian Allan Ramsay explained their purpose:

'Schools polite shall lib'ral Arts display,
And make auld bar'rous Darkness fly away.'

Scottish legal training (a natural choice for young men from good families, and for lowly 'lads o' pairts'), together with university study of European philosophers, helped produce a generation of world-class thinkers and writers, all living or working in Edinburgh. As one admiring English visitor remarked, in 1769: 'Here I stand at what is called the Cross of Edinburgh, and can, in a few minutes, take 50 men of genius by the hand.'

The French, led by famous writer, scientist and philosopher Voltaire, were even more complimentary: 'It is to Scotland that we look for our idea of civilisation.' Out of respect for its great thinkers, Edinburgh also won the nickname 'Athens of the North'.

An A – Z of Edinburgh Intellectuals

William Adam (1684–1748) and **Robert Adam** (1728–1792)
Father and son, both architects. Designed some of the best buildings in Edinburgh New Town (see page 145) and elsewhere in Scotland, plus houses and streets in London. 'Adam' architecture was restrained, regular and elegant, and was inspired by ancient Greek and Roman designs.

Joseph Black (1728–1799)
Physician and scientist, also taught at Glasgow University. Famous for his discoveries of latent heat, specific heat, and carbon dioxide.

Hugh Blair (1718–1800)
Pioneer literary critic, and Scotland's first professor of *'belles lettres'* (the study of language and fine writing). He was also a respected churchman, with moderate, tolerant, charitable opinions.

James Boswell (1740–1795)
Boswell trained as a lawyer, and tried (but failed) to make a career as a British Army officer. In London, he befriended eccentric genius Dr Samuel Johnson, and later wrote a brilliant biography of him. Proud of his native land, he escorted Johnson on a visit to the Scottish Highlands. Boswell's account of their travels, together with his private diaries, are remarkable for their vivid descriptions, psychological insight and personal frankness.

James Burnett, Lord Monboddo (1714–1799)
Brilliant lawyer, judge and philosopher, interested in human origins and the scientific study of languages. A famous eccentric, and founder member of the exclusive Select Society debating club. Members included some of the cleverest men of the age.

Robert Burns (1756–1796)
Handsome, witty, flirtatious Burns came from a poor family in Ayrshire, southwest Scotland. His poems, mostly in Scots, reveal truths about human nature in simple, homely language. They caused a sensation in Edinburgh when they were first published, and Burns became a celebrity. Today, he is Scotland's best-known and best-loved writer.

Adam Fergusson (1723–1816)
Philospher and pioneer sociologist. One of the first to make a scientific study of the way in which people lived. He investigated the beliefs, values and customs of traditional societies (especially in the Scottish Highlands), comparing and contrasting them with the 'modern' life of his day.

Robert Fergusson (no relation) (1750–1774)
One of the first to publish racy, satirical poetry in the Scots language, student Fergusson set an example that was later followed by Burns and others. He died tragically young, poor and neglected, after injuring his brain by falling down stairs.

David Hume (1711–1776)
Philosopher, who created a new 'science of man', studying how humans think, reason, and interpret

the world around them. Hume's ideas challenged religious ideas (Hume did not believe in God) and current political and scientific theories. Today, Hume is still admired as a great and original thinker, especially for his best-known work, *An Enquiry Concerning Human Understanding*.

John Monro (1670–1740)

Army surgeon, and co-founder of Edinburgh's Medical School. It was based on the most advanced colleges of medicine and surgery in continental Europe, especially the Netherlands. With his son, Alexander, a Professor of Anatomy, Monro also founded Edinburgh's first modern hospital (now the Edinburgh Royal Infirmary) in 1737.

John Playfair (1748–1819)

Physicist and mathematician. Keenly interested in astronomy. From a scholarly family, which included architects and engineers. Professor of natural philosophy (= science) at Edinburgh University. He explained the revolutionary ideas of geologist James Hutton to a wider audience.

Sir Henry Raeburn (1756–1823)

Artist, famous for his portraits of proud Scottish noblemen and Highland chiefs. Helped to create an exciting new romantic image of the Scots.

Allan Ramsay, father (1685–1758)

Poet and bookseller; his shop was a meeeting place for intellectuals. He collected and preserved traditional Scots-language songs and poems, and opened Scotland's first lending library in 1725.

Allan Ramsay, son (1713–1784)
Perhaps the greatest Scottish portrait painter. His pictures, especially of women, show great psychological understanding. Also a keen student of literature and philosophy.

William Robertson (1721–1793)
Historian, educator, and leading churchman. He was Principal of Edinburgh University, and encouraged its rapid development. He also served as Moderator (leader) of the Church of Scotland.

Adam Smith (1723–1790)
Nicknamed the 'Father of Modern Economics', Smith also taught moral philosophy (the science of behaviour) at the University of Edinburgh. His best-known work, *An Enquiry into the Nature and Causes of the Wealth of Nations* (1776), is still influential today.

Robert Stevenson (1722–1850)
Founder of a dynasty of expert engineers, who built canals, bridges and over 40 lighthouses in extremely difficult locations. By warning sailors of dangerous rocks and shoals, Stevenson lighthouses saved countless lives at sea.

Dugald Stewart (1753–1783)
Mathematician and philosopher. Taught moral and political philosophy at Edinburgh University, and helped explain the ideas of advanced thinkers to non-academic readers. Viewed with suspicion because he supported the radical ideals (Liberty, Equality, Brotherhood) of the French Revolution of 1789.

Truth springs from argument amongst friends

Are you a genius scientist or revolutionary thinker? Then probably, you get lonely. So why not join Edinburgh's leading men as they meet at their private clubs? Philosopher David Hume explained how he went to the Cape Club (yes, they dressed up) when too much 'speculation' made him depressed:

'since reason is incapable of dispelling these clouds, nature herself suffices to that purpose . . . I dine, I play a game of backgammon, I converse, and am merry with my friends . . .'

Alternative places of good cheer were coffee houses and taverns:

'. . . where ye can get
A crum' o' tripe, ham, dish o' pease,
An egg, or, cauler [fresh] frae the seas
A fluke [flat fish] or whiting [white fish]. . .'

Many of these eating and drinking places were managed by Edinburgh's formidable landladies. (Although one belonged to 'Indian Peter', who had been kidnapped from Aberdeen, sold as a slave, attacked by Native Americans, and captured by French colonists before making his way back to Scotland.) Taverns served simple food at all hours of the day and night - oysters, mutton chops, beef steaks, chicken broth, haggis – and strong drink of all kinds.

A lucky (= landlady)

Close by the door of the kitchen sat Mrs Douglas, a woman of immense bulk, dressed in the most splendid style, with a headdress of stupendous grandeur and a coloured silk gown having daisies flowered on it like sunflowers, and tulips as big as cabbages. She never rose from her seat upon the entry of her guests, either because she was unable from fatness, or that, by sitting, she might preserve the greater dignity. She only bowed to them as they passed, and there were numerous waiters and slip-shod damsels, ready to obey her directions ...

Robert Chambers, Traditions of Edinburgh,
c. 1868

At home

Clubs, taverns and coffeee houses were for men only; no respectable woman would enter. But Edinburgh was also famous as the home of several grand society hostesses. They liked to welcome intellectual or creative celebrities to their drawing rooms, along with male and female members of Edinburgh's best families. Even after 1707, many Scots nobles still kept a town house in Edinburgh – although they spent time in London, as well.

The best-known society hostesses included Eleanor Campbell, Lady Stair (died 1759), who jumped out of a window to escape her violent husband and inspired Sir Walter Scott to write a ghost story, *Aunt Margaret's Mirror*; the famously beautiful Jane Maxwell, Duchess of Gordon, who took a keen interest in the latest farming technology; Helen Hall of Douglas, known as the *lang-heidit lady* for her shrewdness; Christian Ramsay, countess of Dalhousie, a collector of exotic plants; and the extraordinary 'Duchess Kitty' (Catherine, Duchess of Queensberry, died 1777), who dressed in Scottish peasant clothing, kept a pet poet, loved planting trees, got giggles at the royal court, could be unpardonably rude, gave amazing parties, was a loyal wife and kind friend – and died from eating too many cherries.

Lower down the social scale, but intellectually just as impressive, learned ladies such as Alison Rutherford, Mrs Cockburn (1712–1794), held salons (meeting places) for Edinburgh's top writers, thinkers, artists and musicians. Even Robert Burns met his famous sweetheart Clarinda (in real-life, Mrs Agnes MacLehose) at a tea-party held by poetry-loving ladies.

Women in Edinburgh wrote, too. Known as 'Scotland's Jane Austen', Susan Ferrier (1782–1854) mocked the rigid conventions that limited women's lives, and explored fashionable questions about Scotland's past, present and future. Elizabeth Hamilton (1756–1816) helped spread the work of leading Edinburgh thinkers in her books of advice for young women, and wrote pioneering educational studies about how children learn.

Starting all over again

In 1727, English spy Daniel Defoe had remarked:

'I believe, this may be said with Truth, that in no City in the World so many People live in so little Room as at Edinburgh.'

A Tour Through the Whole Island of Great Britain, 1727

By the 1750s, Edinburgh folk and their visitors were talking openly about the need for a New Town. Backed by Edinburgh's Lord Provost, a competition was announced in 1766. It was won by Scottish architect James Craig (1739–1795) and, after much debate and many misgivings, passed for construction the following year.

Edinburgh need not have worried. Although Craig did not live to see many of his planned streets, squares and gardens completed, his design was a resounding success. His idea was simple, but elegant and attractive. He laid out a grid based on three main streets running east to west, with a magnificent square at each end. Craig was not responsible for the buildings constructed there; but fortunately, they are of equal quality to his street-plan. Many were designed by Britain's leading architects, including the Adam family, in restrained, elegant styles inspired by ancient Greece.

To reach the New Town from the original burgh of Edinburgh, now known as the Old Town, the Nor' Loch was drained, and an artifical slope, The Mound, was created from rubble left over from digging New Town foundations. There were also spectacular road bridges: the North, the South, the Regent, and the King George.

Readers, let us leave this chapter as we began it, in company with the Reverend Sydney Smith, as he bids farewell to Edinburgh in 1803:

'Never shall I forget the happy days I spent there amid odious smells, barbarous sounds, bad suppers, excellent hearts and the most enlightened and cultivated understandings.'

Tall slum tenements in Greenside, between
Edinburgh and Leith. By the 19th century,
'an unsavoury haven for the poor'.

CHAPTER FIVE

MINE OWN ROMANTIC TOWN

In 1776, no doubt remembering the horrors of Edinburgh's bloodstained past, economist Adam Smith wrote hopefully that:

'Science is the great antidote to the poison of enthusiasm [religious fanaticism] and superstition.'

Indeed it is, but within a generation of Smith's death in 1790, the people of Edinburgh seemed in danger of forgetting his wise words. Encouraged by local hero, romantic novelist Sir Walter Scott, and a never-ending stream of admiring visitors, they were happy to turn away from Edinburgh's calm, rational 18th-century science, law and medicine. They preferred, instead, to celebrate the romantic natural beauty of its landscape:

'It is the peculiar boast of Edinburgh . . . that nature has done everything, has laid every foundation, and disposed of every line of its rocks and its hills, as if she had designed it for the display of architecture.'

The Edinburgh Review, *1838*

Or else, like passionate English novelist Charlotte Brontë, they liked to imagine Edinburgh as a haunting presence, with more than a hint of the supernatural:

'Who indeed that has once seen Edinburgh, but must see it again in dreams waking or sleeping?'

Even royalty contributed to this collective fantasy. In 1842, Queen Victoria said that the view of Edinburgh, seen from Leith, was 'fairy-like'. Around 20 years earlier, in 1822, her uncle, Britain's King George IV had made a sensational visit to Edinburgh, stage-managed by Sir Walter Scott. Not least because stout King George appeared in a newly invented 'traditional' Scottish outfit, complete with short tartan kilt (which Edinburgh people had never worn) – and pink tights, for modesty. The king was moved to exclaim:

'Good God! What a fine sight. I had no conception there was such a fine scene in the world, and to find it in my own dominions; and the people are as beautiful and extraordinary as the scene.'

All this did Edinburgh's reputation (and good opinion of itself) no harm at all. The tourist industry boomed, all things Scottish became fashionable, and a whole new – largely imaginary – image of Edinburgh was displayed to Scottish people and the rest of the world.

Deeply divided

It took later poets and novelists, such as Chesterton, to claim that underneath all the romantic, tartan, tourist tomfoolery, and behind all the thriving businesses, Edinburgh was still a 'perilous' place. It stood on the edge of moral precipices, as well as geographical ones. Yes, its buildings did soar upwards; the tallest, the 200-feet (61-metre) monument to Sir Walter Scott, completed in 1846, was later nicknamed 'the gothic rocket'. But although Scott's monument looks like a church spire, it did not honour Edinburgh's old God or even 18th-century ideals such as Truth or Justice. Instead, it celebrated the city's spin-doctor; the man who created 'Brand Edinburgh'.

And, yes, Edinburgh Old Town was wonderfully picturesque – so long as you did not look too closely. Its slums were some of the worst in Europe: hungry, overcrowded, criminal, disease-ridden. The New Town was rich, elegant, spacious and airy – but its streets were so wide that neighbours passed by without recognising each other or exchanging normal, friendy, humane greetings. Worst of all, the two halves of the city, old and new, rich and poor, were cut off from each other not only by a deep valley (the drained Nor' Loch, laid out in 1867 as public gardens) but also by deep divisions of wealth, health, class, opportunity and living conditions.

Jekyll and Hyde

A member of the famous engineering dynasty (see page 139), novelist Robert Louis Stevenson (1850–1894) was born in polite New Town Edinburgh. But as a young man and university student, he soon discovered the slums, bars and brothels of Edinburgh's Old Town. In one of his best-known stories, *The Strange Case of Dr Jekyll and Mr Hyde* (1886), the contrast between the two sides of Edinburgh is echoed by the split personality of a respectable doctor who is transformed into a psychopathic monster after drinking a sinister potion.

For over a century, readers have been fascinated by Stevenson's strange tale. And, although *Jekyll and Hyde* is said to be set in London, the text contains descriptions of buildings, streets and nightlife that seem terribly familiar to anyone who knows Edinburgh ...

Yes, readers. While Edinburgh's beautiful New Town was growing fast (by the 1830s, it was the largest planned urban development in the world) and while leafy, healthy, tranquil suburbs were filling the open spaces between Edinburgh and its surrounding villages, original Edinburgh, the Old Town itself, was sinking ever deeper into depravity and despair.

Edinburgh's Old Town saw:

• **Riots**

Some were political protests; some were fights between rival gangs. The most famous was probably the Tron Riot, on New Year's Eve 1811/1812, which combined gang violence and social unrest. It was the custom (and still is) for Edinburgh merry-makers to gather at Hogmanay at the site of the old burgh Tron. But this time, gangs met there to brawl with each other and rob passers-by. A police officer who intervened was brutally murdered. Sixty-eight youths were arrested, and five were sentenced to death.

• Epidemics

Typhus, typhoid, TB, tetanus and dysentery were all common in the Old Town. But the most feared was cholera, which spread across Europe 'like wildfire'. It was carried by dirty water and lack of sanitation – both typically Old Town. And it reached the burgh in 1832 and again in 1848–1849. Although some Edinburgh doctors pioneered new treatments (such as intravenous salt water, which was sensible but ridiculed by the medical establishment), thousands died.

• Fires

In the 1800s, many lands still contained large quantities of wood within their structure – as walls and floors, as doors and windows, as indoor and outdoor stairs, and above all (ha!) as rafters. Fires were common, but by far the worst was in 1824. Then, a candle left burning in a printer's workshop soon set the whole tenement on fire, and the flames quickly spread to buildings 200 yards or more from the start of the blaze. It was three days before they were finally extinguished. Meanwhile, lead roofs melted (so did church bells), over 1,000 men, women and children were made homeless, and 13 people were killed. A whole section of the Old Town was devastated.

Fire was one reason why many tenements collapsed. (The other reasons were shoddy or over-ambitious building.) In 1861, 35 people perished when a land in the High Street crumbled and fell. However, one young boy survived, after rescuers heard him calling: 'Heave awa lads, I'm no deid yet!'

• **Overcrowding**
For centuries, Edinburgh's population had been steadily growing, but in the 19th century it increased dramatically:

c. 1600	8,000
c. 1700	35,000
c. 1750	49,000
1811	82,000
1831	135,000
1851	345,000

Some of this increase was due to the New Town and the new suburbs. Some was due to the take-over by Edinburgh of small villages nearby – even the port of Leith, later, in 1920.

But most of it was due to immigration – from the surrounding farmland, from elsewhere in Scotland, from across the North Sea, from Italy, and especially from Ireland, as starving families fled to escape the potato famine of the 1840s. Many immigrants did find the jobs they longed for, but others joined Edinburgh's underclass – or underworld.

Underclass, underworld, underground

After weathly, well-educated families moved away to the New Town or to new suburbs, the Old Town of Edinburgh was no longer inhabited by its traditional mix of 'all manner and conditions of men' (and women). Instead, it became a ghetto, for the weak, feeble, helpless, hopeless or simply poor – and for criminals.

All these unfortunates were crowded together in the Cowgate – once the home to great lords and ladies, now one of Britain's worst slums. Or else they made their homes in the damp, dingy rabbit-warren of cellars and basements that ran beneath Old Town tenements.

Burke and Hare

Edinburgh doctors were world famous, and so was its medical school. And how did the students learn? By cutting up dead bodies. Where did these bodies come from? Shhh! Don't ask! You really want to know? Well, whisper it quietly: from the 'resurrection men' – grave-robbers, who crept out at dead of night to remove newly buried corpses from Edinburgh tombs.

Selling bodies was a lucrative, if grisly, business. So in 1828, two Irish labourers, who had come to Edinburgh to find work, set up a nastly little private enterprise. They invited drunks, down and outs, abandoned women, to their Old Town lodgings – and smothered them. Then they sold the bodies, mostly to Dr Knox, a superstar anatomy teacher. They killed at least 16 known victims before they were caught, maybe many more. Hare turned King's Evidence; Burke was hanged – and his body was cut up for medical research, just like his victims'.

The good doctors

In 1852, Old Town doctor George Bell surveyed the living conditions of some of his patients. He wrote:

'We return day after day and night after night, to the scenes of misery, disease and death. We listen to the cry of the children, the wail of the women, the deep utterances of men . . . What can we do?'

Thankfully, help was at hand:

• **Dr Henry Littlejohn**, appointed Edinburgh's first Medical Officer of Health in 1862, demanded that the worst Old Town slums be pulled down, vaccinated children against smallpox, and set up Edinburgh's first Hospital for Sick Children in 1860.

Littlejohn was also Edinburgh's chief police surgeon, helping to solve crimes and appearing in court – with great drama – to prosecute criminals. Together with Edinburgh surgeon **Dr Joseph Bell**, he inspired Edinburgh-born doctor-novelist Sir Arthur Conan Doyle

(1859–1930) to create his famous detective, Sherlock Holmes. Bell was said to be able to discern a person's occupation, and more, simply by looking at them. Holmes's arch-enemy Moriarty was inspired by Edinburgh University student – and serial killer – Thomas Cream.

Higher up the social scale:

• Surgeon **Joseph Lister** (1827–1912) taught at Edinburgh University and saved millions of lives by pioneering techniques of antiseptic surgery.

• **James Simpson** (1811–1870) discovered the anaesthetic properties of chloroform – by experimenting on himself and his friends. He later gave anaesthetics to Queen Victoria, during the birth of three of her nine children. Away from his celebrity patients, Simpson also helped run a dispensary for poor people in Edinburgh's Old Town.

What about the women?

Surprisingly for such a genteel place, middle-class Edinburgh was one of the earliest – and most important – centres of feminist protest in Britain. Large numbers of women turned their backs on conventional domesticity, and joined organisations such as the Scottish Women's Suffrage Society (which called for votes for women – and poor men – and met for the first time in 1867) and the Edinburgh Ladies' Emancipation Society, which campaigned for an end to slavery. There were also women's pressure groups calling for temperance (a ban on alcohol, combined with moral reform, especially for the poor), better educational opportunities, and international peace.

Wealthy women, such as best-selling children's novelist Catherine Sinclair (1800–1864), gave large sums to fund 'missions' that combined religious teaching with welfare work in the poorest parts of Edinburgh. Sinclair also gave pensions to poor elderly people, set up an industrial school to train slum girls for careers as respectable domestic servants, built public drinking fountains to provide clean water and set up 'cooking depots' (cheap public canteens).

Edinburgh women also worked to improve medical care for female patients. They included:

• **Sophia Jex Blake** (1840–1912), who fought long and hard to become the first female in Britain to attend medical school alongside men, and the first to qualify as a doctor. (Edinburgh's Miranda 'James' Barry had trained and served as an Army surgeon from the 1810s to the 1860s – but she had lived her life disguised as a man, so that is rather a different story...)

• **Elsie Inglis** (1864–1917) campaigned tirelessly for improved medical care for Edinburgh's women, and led a team of volunteer women doctors and nurses on World War I battlefields.

On the other hand ...

For anyone with money, Edinburgh could be a very pleasant place to live. And, from around 1800, that money came from industry, as well as Edinburgh's old-style trades and professions. Although, compared with the shipbuilding, iron and chemical works in Glasgow, Scotland's biggest city, Edinburgh's industries were lightweight, they were still profitable. They've been summed up in three words: books, brewing and biscuits, but a fourth should also be added: banking. To a lesser extent, there was pottery and glassmaking, and ironworking, too.

Edinburgh bankers, stockbrokers and insurance underwriters helped arrange the finance for new industries in many parts of Scotland; they also served famously frugal Scots savers. The Edinburgh book trade included publishers as well as booksellers – and, of course, encyclopaedias. (The *Encylopaedia Britannica* had been founded in the burgh in 1768, and was still going strong.) And the tourist industry grew and grew, not only in Edinburgh's stunning centre, but also in seaside suburbs such as Joppa and Portobello. At Leith, the docks were rebuilt – although this cost so much that it temporarily bankrupted the burgh council.

Edinburgh industries created jobs – for clerks, technicians, factory hands, maintenance workers, cooks and cleaners. The thousands of new families living in the burgh also needed a willing workforce: builders, gardeners, handymen, decorators, coach and cab drivers, street cleaners, lamplighters, delivery boys, schoolteachers, doctors and nurses, shop assistants, park-keepers and a whole army of domestic servants.

And, of course, all these people – employers and servants – spent their money in Edinburgh, on everything from basic foodstuffs to luxury furnishings. In the New Town, elegant shops, including department stores – the latest fashion – and smart hotels lined Princes Street; in the suburbs and the Old Town, family-run butchers, bakers, ironmongers and greengrocers, stationers, chemists and drapers stood on smart and shabby street corners.

Britain's favourite biscuit

It's been said that, today, 52 chocolate digestive biscuits are eaten every second. Goodness knows how they know, but the fact would certainly have surprised young Alexander Grant, a worker at the Edinburgh bakery of McVitie and Price, who created a new kind of biscuit in 1892 – and called it 'digestive'. Why the worthy, semi-medical name? Because Grant's recipe contained a goodly amount of bicarbonate of soda, often used as a home remedy for upset stomachs.

... and the author's un-favourite sweetie!

Loved by many, but strongly disliked by this writer, it's Edinburgh's own special treat: Edinburgh Rock. Not tasted it yet? It's dry, smooth, powdery and melts in the mouth in an extraordinary fashion. Invented by burgh confectioner Alexander Ferguson, nicknamed 'Sweetie Sandy', in the early 19th century, Edinburgh Rock contains just sugar, water, cream of tartar and flavourings. Traditionally it's tinted: pink (raspberry), white (vanilla), fawn (ginger) and yellow (orange or lemon). And packed in tartan boxes – what else?

Sweetie Sandy was not the only inventive Edinburgh citizen in the 19th century. Politicians, scientists, doctors, engineers and business people of all kinds were very, very busy. . .

Politics

1792 First Meeting of Friends of the People Society, in support of the French Revolution. Leaders were transported.

1811–1812 Tron Riot (see page 152)

1812 Edinburgh Police Act introduces more street police patrols.

1814 Protest meeting calling for an end to slavery in the Caribbean.

1814 Edinburgh Castle no longer used for war, or as a military prison. Instead, it is declared a national monument and its buildings are slowly restored.

1822 Building work starts on National Monument (in ancient Greek style) on Calton Hill, to commemorate soldiers and sailors killed in the wars against French emperor Napoleon. Work stops when money runs out in 1829.

1824 Edinburgh Fire Establishment founded – the first council fire service in Britain.

1832 Demonstrations by townspeople in support of the 1832 Reform Bill (which gave more men the right to vote).

1833 City government is bankrupt after financing new docks at Leith.

1842 Queen Victoria visits Edinburgh during her first tour of Scotland; orders Holyrood Palace (then partly ruined) to be restored as a royal family home.

1853 Edinburgh Trades Council (Association of Trades Unions) set up, to represent working people.

1856 Canongate district becomes part of the burgh of Edinburgh.

1864 Last public execution in Edinburgh, in the Lawnmarket.
1867 Edinburgh City Improvement Act; rebuilding of Old Town begins.
1896 Village of Portobello becomes part of the burgh of Edinburgh.

A postcard view of 19th-century Edinburgh

Arts and sciences

1800 National Museum of Antiquities established.

1802 *Edinburgh Review* (literary and political magazine) first published.

1817 First issue of *The Scotsman* daily newspaper.

1817 *Blackwood's Magazine* (rival to the *Edinburgh Review*) founded.

1818 New astronomical observatory built on Calton Hill.

1820 Work begins on new Botanic Garden, at Leith.

1822 First Highland and Agricultural Show (held near Edinburgh).

1825–1827 Charles Darwin (yes, evolution!) studies at Edinburgh University.

1826 Royal Insitution (founded in 1783 for 'the advancement of learning and useful knowledge') moves to its new building on The Mound (see page 145).

1826 Royal Scottish Academy (of Fine Art) is founded.

1827 Sir Walter Scott admits to being the author of the Waverly Novels (as a gentleman, he had originally published them anonymously).

1841–1851 Donaldson's Hospital for the Deaf is opened.

1859 National Gallery of Scotland opens.

1879 Watt Institution and School of Arts founded (later, Heriot-Watt University).

1883 Royal Lyceum Theatre opens.

1890 Central Library opens; it is free to the public.

1895 Royal National Observatory built on Blackford Hill.

1906 King's Theatre opens.

Trade, transport and industry

1802–1817 Old wooden luckenbooths (wooden lock-up market stalls) removed from High Street.

1806 Grand Head Office built for Bank of Scotland.

1818 Building work starts on the Union Canal to link Edinburgh and Falkirk (home of great iron foundries).

1818 First gas lighting in Edinburgh.

1819 Regular daily horse-drawn coach service between Edinburgh and Glasgow.

1822 Union Canal opens.

1822 Princes Street's old oil-lamps replaced by gas lighting.

1824 Great Fire of Edinburgh destroys homes, shops and workshops in the Old Town.

1831 Edinburgh to Dalkeith railway opens; carriages are pulled along rails by horses (later, by steam locomotives).

1842 Edinburgh to Glasgow railway line opens.

1846 North British Railway founded.

1848 Waverley Railway Station built.

1861 The One o'clock Gun is fired from Edinburgh Castle for the first time. It is a time-signal for ships at Leith and the Firth of Forth.

1862 Flying Scotsman train service; reaches London in ten and a half hours.

1871 First horse-drawn trams.

1883–1890 Construction of Forth Road Bridge, at Queensferry. It is 2 km long, carries a railway track 48 m above the water, and uses over 54,000 tons of steel. Fifty-three workmen die building it.

1886 Edinburgh International Exhibition to encourage trade and manufactures.

1910 First electric trams.

Pride of fair Scotland

A poet so bad that he's often hailed as a genius, William Topaz McGonagall was born in Edinburgh to Irish parents, in either 1825 or 1830. He moved to Dundee, worked as a handloom weaver, performed as an amateur actor, and gave readings of his 'poetic gems' on the streets, in bars and public halls, and even at the circus. He died in poverty, back in Edinburgh, in 1902.

Here's what he had to say about his birthplace:

Beautiful city of Edinburgh, most wonderful to be
   seen,
With your ancient palace of Holyrood and Queen's
   Park Green,
And your big, magnificent, elegant New College,
Where people from all nations can be taught
   knowledge.

The New College of Edinburgh is certainly very
   grand
Which I consider to be an honour to fair Scotland,
Because it's the biggest in the world, without any
   doubt,
And is most beautiful in the inside as well as out.

And the Castle is wonderful to look upon,
Which has withstood many angry tempests in years
   bygone;
And the rock it's built upon is rugged and lovely
   to be seen
When the shrubberies surrounding it are blown
   full green.

Morningside [a 'refined' suburb] is lovely and
  charming to be seen;
The gardens there are rich with flowers and
  shrubberies green
And sweet scented perfumes fill the air,
Emanating from the sweet flowers and beautiful
  plants there.

And as for Braidhill [see page 25], it's a very
  romantic spot,
But a fine place to visit when the weather is hot;
There the air is nice and cool, which will help to
  drive away sorrow
When ye view from its summit the beautiful city of
  Edinburgh.

And as for the statues, they are very grand –
They cannot be surpassed in any foreign land;
And the scenery is attractive and fascinating to the
  eye,
And arrests the attention of tourists as they
  pass by.

Lord Melville's Monument is most elegant to be
  seen,
Which is situated in St. Andrew's Square, amongst
  shrubberies green,
Which seems most gorgeous to the eye,
Because it is towering so very high.

The Prince Albert Consort Statue looks very
  grand,
Especially the granite blocks whereon it doth
  stand,

Which is admired by all tourists as they pass by,
Because the big granite blocks seem magnificent to
the eye.

Princes Street West End Garden is fascinating to
be seen,
With its beautiful big trees and shrubberies green,
And its magnificent water fountain in the valley
below
Helps to drive away from the tourist all care and
woe.

The Castle Hotel is elegant and grand,
And students visit it from every foreign land,
And the students of Edinburgh often call there
To rest and have luncheon, at a very cheap fare.

Queen Street Garden seems charming to the eye,
And a great boon it is to the tenantry near by,
As they walk along the grand gravel walks near
there,
Amongst the big trees and shrubberies, and inhale
pure air.

Then, all ye tourists, be advised by me,
Beautiful Edinburgh ye ought to go and see.
It's the only city I know of where ye can wile away
the time
By viewing its lovely scenery and statues fine.

Magnificent city of Edinburgh, I must conclude
my muse,
But to write in praise of thee I cannot refuse.
I will tell the world boldly without dismay

You have the biggest college in the world at the
  present day.
Of all the cities in the world, Edinburgh for me;
For no matter where I look, some lovely spot I see;
And for picturesque scenery unrivalled you do
  stand.
Therefore I pronounce you to be the Pride of Fair
  Scotland.

*William Topaz McGonagall, 'Beautiful
Edinburgh', from* Poetic Gems Selected from
the Works of William McGonagall, Poet and
Tragedian, with Biographical Sketch by the
Author and Portrait, *1890*

'Stop the world,
Scotland wants to get on.'

*Senior MSP Winnie Ewing, grande dame of
Scottish Nationalists, 1967*

CHAPTER SIX

BACK TO THE FUTURE

A h Edimbra, Edinbroo! What to say about your recent past, your present, and your future? What are you doing now? How do you want to be remembered?

Perhaps, surprisingly, as the home of Scotland's most militant suffragettes, where 9-year-old bagpipe player Bessie Watson led protest marches in 1909 to call for votes for women? As the city that German zeppelin airships tried to bomb (in 1916), but miraculously missed? As the birthplace of novelist Muriel Spark's sly, ungenerous, ambivalent Miss Jean Brodie?

(Published in 1961, the book looks back to the 1930s). As the hang-out of poets who fought to restore Scots as a highbrow literary language – most laudably, but incomprehensibly to many ordinary Scottish people?

Or should we think of Edinburgh as the place where, in the 1950s, a handsome young ex-milkman named Thomas Sean Connery posed naked as a life-model for art students? As the urban jungle of Irvine Welsh's witty, foul-mouthed *Trainspotting* (novel 1993, film 1996), where hopes are kept alive, then killed, by sex'n'drugs'n'alcohol? Or even as just one of 30 cities with the same name (those Scottish colonists got everywhere), from Australia to Zimbabwe? To say nothing of places named 'Dunedin'...

Perhaps we should remember Edinburgh as the city that let the Old Town fade away and become a deserted slum by the 1950s? Or as the place where – very nearly – a 1960s motorway was built right through its centre? Or, like countless comedians, spouting stereotypes, should we think of Edinburgh as the home of mean, narrow-minded folk who prefer to assume that 'You'll have had your tea...'[1] or where the outward show of prosperous respectability can hide something very different. For example, the weird and wonderful seances, led by Scotswoman Helen Duncan: 17 stone, given to hysterics, and the last British woman to be imprisoned for practising magic – and fraud, in 1944?

Or, Fair Edina, is all this mockery wildly out of order? Would you rather be remembered for happier achievements? If so, let's turn to look at the later 20th century, and the early years of this one. They have, to be honest, been pretty impressive:

• First the Festival, founded in 1947 to provide 'a platform for the flowering of the human spirit' (no less), and now acclaimed as one of the top cultural events anywhere on the globe. International, eclectic, pioneering. Sometimes controversial; often really, really good.

---

1. *The Glasgow equivalent is almost always 'C'mon in.' Yes, honestly...*

Bigger and better? The Festival Fringe: almost a month of comedy – and anything else in the performance line that you'd care to imagine. Noisier, wilder, stranger, year by year; sometimes rubbish and sometimes mind-blowingly original.

Not forgetting the Edinburgh Book Festival, Film Festival, Science Festival, Mela (South Asian Festival), and much more...

• Secondly, the SNP – the Scottish National Party. Although founded in Glasgow (in 1934), its headquarters have long been in Edinburgh. And, since the Scottish Parliament was reconvened in 1999 (after a wait of almost 300 years), so have its main political activities. Like it or loathe it, the SNP is now a force to be reckoned with in Scottish politics, and Edinburgh once again has a thriving political culture.

• Thirdly, those blockbuster storytellers: yes, of course, J. K. Rowling, of Harry Potter fame. At least two Edinburgh cafés claim to be the place where, as a penniless single mother, she wrote the first of her epic fantasies.

Although many names, and some buildings, in Rowling's stories seem to have been inspired by Edinburgh originals, the city itself does not feature strongly in her books. The opposite is true of Edinburgh's other current literary success: a tremendous sense of place inspires Ian Rankin's tough Inspector Rebus detective novels and TV series. By around 2010, Rankin's books accounted for one in every ten crime novels purchased in Britain.

• Fourth, a sci-fi sheep. Yes, hello Dolly, and hello a brave new world of genetic engineering. In 1996, Professor Ian Wilmut – now a Nobel prizewinner – became the first person successfully to clone living offspring from an adult mammal cell. And he did so at the Roslin Institute, part of Edinburgh University. Dolly herself lived until 2003, and is now on display (alas, so stuffed and primped as to look hardly real) at the National Museum of Scotland, in Edinburgh.

• Fifth, hooray for heritage. Edinburgh's well-preserved past is largely thanks to the tourist industry. Visitors flock to see a city declared to be of World Heritage importance. Before that accolade was awarded, local volunteer groups worked to oppose some of the 1960s and 1970s planners' most destructive schemes. What we owe them is incalculable. Today Edinburgh has the rare distinction of being a city where people love living in the restored, historic centre; they commute out to work, rather than travelling in.

Above all, Edinburgh is a city that seems to have the knack of reinventing itself: from tribal fortress to bustling market, royal capital, stern righteous commonwealth, look-ahead place of learning (and pleasure), romantic refuge, prim backwater, and vibrant cultural centre for visitors from all round the world. With such a past and present, who knows what Edinburgh's future has in store?

Ten more things to thank Edinburgh for

We've read about some Edinburgh achievements, but we can thank the burgh and its inhabitants for much, much more:

1. **The telephone** (1876). Alexander Graham Bell began his experiments on sound and hearing in Edinburgh.
2. **Pirate films and fashions.** Long John Silver, first pirate anti-hero, was created by Robert Louis Stevenson in *Treasure Island* (1883).
3. **Geology.** In 1785, scientist James Hutton explained how rocks were formed, and that the Earth was many millions of years old.
4. **The decimal point.** Devised by mathematician John Napier in 1616. He also invented logarithms.
5. **Colour Photography.** The three-colour process (mixing red, green and blue light) was invented by James Clerk Maxwell in 1855.
6. **Hypodermic syringes.** Invented by Edinburgh doctor Alexander Wood in 1853.
7. **Electronics.** In 1862, James Clerk Maxwell explained electromagnetism, and paved the way for today's mass communications, computers and many other devices.
8. **Clinical trials of medicines** – and a cure for scurvy. Pioneered in 1747 by Edinburgh-born surgeon James Lind.
9. **Historical novels.** The first, *Waverley*, was written by Sir Walter Scott in 1814.
10. **Life-saving bacteria** that detect hidden explosives, genetically engineered by Edinburgh University scientists in 2009.

One Edinburgh yard and its dog

How to sum up? Over the centuries, Edinburgh has been so many things to so many different people. Where better to pause and think about them all than tree-shaded Greyfriars Kirkyard? In its own way, this peaceful patch of ground, just south of the busy, noisy High Street, tells Edinburgh's story in miniature.

At first, the yard was the garden of a Franciscan friary. When that was destroyed in 1559, Greyfriars became a burial ground. Zealous Presbyerians met there in 1638 to sign the National Covenant. In 1679, a thousand were imprisoned close to the tombs, in terrible conditions. The ghost of their persecutor, 'Bluidy' George Mackenzie (died 1681), is still said to attack visitors.

In the 18th and 19th centuries, many of Edinburgh's great thinkers were laid to rest at Greyfriars, in tombs as elegant as their intellects. And lesser graves were fitted with 'mortsafes' (iron cages) to defeat body-snatchers! Photographers Robert Adamson and David Octavius Hill crouched among the monuments in the 1840s, capturing faint, poignant images. Soon after, along came a certain Skye terrier, Greyfriars Bobby. It was said that Bobby sat by his dead master's grave for 14 years (1858–1872). Hundreds came to admire; even Queen Victoria was impressed by his devotion. Recent research suggests that 'Bobby' may have been two different dogs, or more. An early example of Edinburgh profiting from the tourist industry?

Today members of the Highland Kirk meet to worship at Greyfriars – a reminder that many immigrants from other parts of Scotland once came to seek work or education in Edinburgh. The city is also a venue for international arts and culture, and offers help and training to some of Edinburgh's most disadvantaged people.

Glossary

apparel To dress, decorate or provide furnishings.

auld (as in *Auld Reekie*; Scots) Old.

ballistics The scientific study of weapons.

bannocks Flat cakes, baked on a hot stone or iron griddle (thick plate) over a fire.

basalt A hard, dark-coloured stone, formed from cooling volcanic lava.

bronze A metal alloy (mixture) of copper and tin.

Bronze Age A name used by historians to describe the centuries when bronze-smelting was a people's most important technology. In Scotland, the Bronze Age lasted from around 3000 to 750 BC.

burgh Originally (1) a fortified settlement. Later (2) a town with trading privileges granted by a king or powerful noble.

cachet (French) Added status or attraction.

Celtic The name used by historians to describe the peoples who lived in western and central Europe from around 800 BC to AD 300. It is also used to describe their languages, lifestyle, art and culture.

chastity Moral and sexual purity.

cholera A deadly disease that causes severe diarrhoea and vomiting. Carried by polluted water.

chroniclers Early historians, who recorded important events in day-by-day order.

civet A species of wild cat. In the past, a smelly substance produced by glands near civet-cats' tails was a valuable ingredient in perfumes.

GLOSSARY

clients (in politics) Weaker people who agree to co-operate with a stronger power. In return, they receive protection.

closes In Edinburgh, narrow alleyways with tall buildings on either side.

damsels Young girls or women.

deduce Prove or understand by looking closely at evidence.

discourse Discussions, conversation.

douce (Scots) Gentle, mild, polite, well-behaved.

dreich (Scots) Cold, grey, miserable, grim. Used to describe the weather.

ducking stool A chair fixed to a crane or similar device, used to punish minor crimes or to try and detect more serious offences. An accused person was sat on the stool, and then dipped in deep water.

dun (also spelled *din*; Celtic) A hilltop fort.

ecclesiastical Connected with the organisation of the Christian Church.

eminence High place.

erroneously Wrongly.

firth River estuary.

forbear To stop or hesitate.

gandiegow (Scots) Heavy rainfall, downpour.

haar (Scots) Thick sea-mist.

hammermen Skilled, trained, metalworkers.

Hogmanay (Scots) New Year's Eve.

impiety Disrespect for religion.

Iron Age A name used by historians to describe the centuries when iron-smelting was a people's most important technology. In Scotland, the Iron Age lasted from around 700 BC to AD 500.

183

keep The strong central building of a castle. Often shaped liked a tower.

King's (or Queen's) Evidence Testimony from a criminal who confesses to their crime and provides information to help convict their accomplices. In return, they often receive a reduced punishment or a pardon.

knight In medieval Europe, a high-ranking warrior who fought on horseback.

lands The name given to tall tenements (apartment blocks) in Edinburgh.

midden Heap of refuse or rubbish.

patronage Protection and support (often financial) from a stronger person or group.

pinhole camera A simple camera without a lens. It consists of a lightproof box with a small hole on one side. It can project an upside-down image on a screen, or be connected to light-sensitive film, to produce photographs.

plype (Scots) Heavy rainfall.

reekie (Scots) Smoky, smelly.

retinues Groups of followers.

Royal Mile The modern name given to the streets that lead from Edinburgh Castle to Holyrood Palace. From west to east: Castlehill, Lawnmarket, High Street, Canongate, Abbey Strand.

snell (Scots) Bitterly cold.

squire Young man, living in the European Middle Ages, working as a trainee knight and/or personal assistant to a knight.

GLOSSARY

tanners Workers who process raw animal hides and turn them into leather. In past times, a messy, smelly, dirty, disease-ridden job.

Tattoo A military display of music and marching, held every year close to Edinburgh Castle. The name is said to come from the Dutch 'tap-toe', which means 'shut the taps' [on the beer-barrels]. In other words, a command to soldiers: 'Go back to your barracks for the night.'

temperance Soberness, moderation.

toft A narrow strip of land.

tolbooth A building where taxes and tolls (charges for importing, exporting, buying and selling) were collected. In the past, often also used as a meeting place for local government officials. In Edinburgh, a prison, as well.

Trades (in Edinburgh) Organised groups of skilled, trained workers.

tron A large balance (set of scales) used for weighing goods on sale in a public market. Used to help prevent fraud.

vengeance Revenge.

viol Early musical instrument, with strings and played with a bow.

warie (Scots) Hard, bleak.

weel-respectit (Scots) Well-respected.

whetstones Very hard, fine-grained stones. Used to rub against metal weapons and tools to produce a sharp cutting edge.

wynds Narrow lanes or alleyways.

Index

Very Peculiar Histories™

at The Cherished Library

History of the British Isles
England (in 3 volumes)
   Vol. 1: From Ancient Times to Agincourt
     David Arscott   978-1-908973-37-5
   Vol. 2: From the Wars of the Roses to the
     Industrial Revolution *Ian Graham*   978-1-908973-38-2
   Vol. 3: From Trafalgar to the New Elizabethans
     John Malam   978-1-908973-39-9
   Boxed set of all three English volumes: 978-1-908973-41-2
Scotland (in 2 volumes) *Fiona Macdonald*
   Vol. 1: From Ancient Times to Robert the Bruce
      978-1-906370-91-6
   Vol. 2: From the Stewarts to Modern Scotland
      978-1-906714-79-6
   Boxed set of both Scottish volumes: 978-1-909645-03-5
   Ireland *Jim Pipe*   978-1-905638-98-7
   Wales *Rupert Matthews*   978-1-907184-19-2

History of the 20th century
Titanic *Jim Pipe*   978-1-907184-87-1
World War One *Jim Pipe*   978-1-908177-00-1
World War Two *Jim Pipe*   978-1-908177-97-1
The Blitz *David Arscott*   978-1-907184-18-5
Rations *David Arscott*   978-1-907184-25-3
The 60s *David Arscott*   978-1-908177-92-6

Social history
Victorian Servants *Fiona Macdonald*   978-1-907184-49-9

North of the Border
Edinburgh *Fiona Macdonald*   978-1-908973-82-5
Scottish Clans *Fiona Macdonald*   978-1-908759-90-0
Scottish Tartan and Highland Dress
   Fiona Macdonald   978-1-908759-89-4
Scottish Words *Fiona Macdonald*   978-1-908759-63-4
Whisky *Fiona Macdonald*   978-1-907184-76-5

Folklore and traditions
Christmas *Fiona Macdonald* 978-1-907184-50-5
Vampires *Fiona Macdonald* 978-1-907184-39-0
Heroes, Gods and Monsters of Celtic Mythology
  Fiona Macdonald 978-1-905638-97-0

British places
Brighton *David Arscott* 978-1-906714-89-5
Edinburgh *Fiona Macdonald* 978-1-908973-82 5
London *Jim Pipe* 978-1-907184-26-0
Oxford *David Arscott* 978-1-908973-81-8
Yorkshire *John Malam* 978-1-907184-57-4

Famous Britons
Great Britons *Ian Graham* 978-1-907184-59-8
Robert Burns *Fiona Macdonald* 978-1-908177-71-1
Charles Dickens *Fiona Macdonald* 978-1-908177-15-5
William Shakespeare *Jacqueline Morley* 978-1-908177-15-5

Sports and pastimes
Cricket *Jim Pipe* 978-1-908177-90-2
Fishing *Rob Beattie* 978-1-908177-91-9
Golf *David Arscott* 978-1-907184-75-8
The Olympics *David Arscott* 978-1-907184-78-9
The World Cup *David Arscott* 978-1-907184-38-3

Royalty
Kings & Queens of Great Britain
  Antony Mason 978-1-906714-77-2
Royal Weddings *Fiona Macdonald* 978-1-907184-84-0
The Tudors *Jim Pipe* 978-1-907184-58-1
Queen Elizabeth II Diamond Jubilee:
  60 Years a Queen *David Arscott* 978-1-908177-50-6

Natural history
Cats *Fiona Macdonald* 978-1-908973-34-4
Dogs *Fiona Macdonald* 978-1-908973-35-1
Global Warming *Ian Graham* 978-1-907184-51-2

Ancient and medieval history
Ancient Egypt: Mummy Myth and Magic
  Jim Pipe 978-1-906714-92-5
Castles *Jacqueline Morley* 978-1-907184-48-2

This is Volume 45 of A Very Peculiar History at The Cherished Library. A list of authors and their works in this series will be found on the preceding pages. The publishers will be pleased to send freely to all applicants an illustrated catalogue of the Library and our many other publications.

Book House
25 Marlborough Place
Brighton
BN1 1UB

www.salariya.com

Some reviews of other volumes in this series

Queen Elizabeth II Diamond Jubilee by David Arscott

'In a nutshell, this is a pocket sized book in the style of a magazine, crammed with interesting titbits of the royal family . . . it is a fun read and genuinely something for everyone.'

Regency Magazine

Whisky by Fiona Macdonald

'Good-humoured, well researched. . .'

Ian Buxton

Libberton Wynd, Old Town